Old American
Kitchenware

1725–1925

Old American
Kitchenware
1725–1925

Louise K. Lantz

Published jointly by

Thomas Nelson Inc.

CAMDEN   NEW YORK

and

Everybodys Press

HANOVER, PENNSYLVANIA

TO MONICA
AND MARK

children of today
with an appreciation
of yesterday

Sixth Printing

© *1970 by Louise K. Lantz*

All rights reserved. Published in Nashville, Tennessee, by Thomas Nelson Inc., and in Hanover, Pennsylvania, by Everybodys Press, and simultaneously in Don Mills, Ontario, by Thomas Nelson & Sons (Canada) Limited.

Design by Harold Leach

ISBN 0-8407-4317-3

Library of Congress Catalog Card Number 75–101527

PRINTED IN THE UNITED STATES OF AMERICA

Acknowledgments

Although my intense interest in old American kitchenware has been accepted by many as a harmless idiosyncracy, there are a few who have shared or nurtured my enthusiasm. First, many thanks to Marcia Ray for years of encouragement and gentle prodding. Without Marcia, this book would never have been. Many thanks to my good friend, Mary Keefer, for the loan of pieces from her vast antique collections and for her shared information; to my parents, Nicholas and Anna Kalaman, who were really the beginning of it all; to my father-in-law, Charles Edward Lantz, a storehouse of information and, as Willafred Studios, the excellent photographer of some of my illustrations; and, last in order but first in my mind, my husband, Curtis Edward Lantz, who photographed all the illustrations not otherwise credited.

Next, I must express my appreciation to the following magazines for permission to reprint my articles and photographs originally published by them: *Spinning Wheel, Hobbies, The Antiques Journal.*

Finally, my sincere thanks to the following museums, restorations, publishers, and business firms for photographs and assistance:

Aluminum Company of America
Art Institute of Chicago
The Bennington Museum
The Buten Museum of Wedgwood
Colonial Williamsburg
Crown Publishers
Henry Francis du Pont Winterthur Museum
Imperial Oil Limited
Lincoln Home State Memorial
The Metropolitan Museum of Art
Morgan Woodwork Organization
Mystic Seaport
National Gallery of Art
Philadelphia Museum of Art
The Rusty Naill, Ellie and Bill Naill, owners
Shelburne Museum, Inc.
Union Carbide Corporation

Preface

Collecting old American kitchenware is a rapidly expanding national hobby. Young and old, male and female, institutions and individuals, all are lured by the charm of old kitchenware. Business firms, such as bakeries and canning companies, are establishing their own collections of antique kitchen utensils. Interior decorators and homemakers, too, are discovering the interest in and attractiveness of these kitchen artifacts. More and more museums, restorations, and historical associations are adding kitchenware to their collections. Even garden clubs and flower-arranging groups are turning to old kitchen implements for unusual containers for their fruits and flowers.

The appeal of kitchen antiques is in their simplicity and their intimate association with the lives of their original users. One wonders who cranked this apple peeler, how happy or sad was the lot of the child who pumped that churn, or what woman lifted that heavy pot. Kitchenware was a part of everyday existence, unlike a silver saltcellar or a cut crystal bowl which was for special-day use only. Old kitchenware bears the marks of usage—scratches on tinware, dents in copper, cracks in pottery—the visages of a productive life.

Besides in the usual antiques shops, kitchenware collectibles may be discovered in Goodwill and Salvation Army stores, thrift shops, second-hand shops, auctions, rummage sales, and at the white-elephant tables of church and school bazaars. Ads placed in antique-collectors' magazines and newspapers assist in locating specific items. Since kitchenware is considered mundane by the uninitiated, bargains are still available. However, these objects are becoming more scarce and more costly each day, as the number of kitchenware collectors increases.

From the primitive relics of the days of fireplace cookery to the quaint accessories for the Victorian coal stove to the rudimentary utensils of the newfangled electric range, collecting old kitchenware is fascinating and worth while. As the demand for old kitchenware increases, as new collectors are initiated, and as veteran collectors search diligently for rare items, the price of old kitchenware rises. The number of kitchenware articles produced by factories, local blacksmiths, tinsmiths, and coopers, and by the dexterous, ingenious farmer must have reached the millions. Some of these items have been discarded, others are still being used for their original purposes, many have found a loving home in a museum or private collection. Appreciation of the elegancies of past eras has been persistent; appreciation of the tools of daily household living has just begun.

Contents

The kitchen of the Governor's Palace in Williamsburg has been reconstructed and today is open in connection with the Governor's Palace, one of the major exhibition buildings in the restored eighteenth-century Virginia capital. Costumed attendants are on hand in the kitchen to describe the furnishings and to demonstrate methods of cooking used 200 years ago. *From Colonial Williamsburg*

Some of the kitchen utensils in an eighteenth-century kitchen appear cumbersome in size and intriguing in shape when compared with those of the twentieth century. From the lackluster of the heavy, dark ironware to the subdued glint of pewter to the warm glow of sunny brass and copper, these venerable kitchen furnishings seem strange, yet warm and homelike, to the modern observer.

The eighteenth-century kitchen itself was either a back room of the house, as in Williamsburg's George Wythe's house, or a completely separate outbuilding, as in George Washington's Mount Vernon. The essential fireplace, around which the kitchen functioned, dominated the early American kitchen with its huge size and ample hearth. It was most often built of brick, occasionally of stone, and the fire was kept burning continuously with whatever wood was locally available. Then, as now, hickory and apple wood were favored for roasting and broiling. Sometimes large fire-backs of iron with attractive raised designs were placed at the back of the fireplace to reflect the heat and to prevent the crumbling of the brick or stone backs from the intense heat of the constant year-round fires. Some of the early fireplaces were so huge as to have seats built within them on the sides, which were favorite resting spots for children and the elderly alike. What a cozy spot on a cold winter's night!

The floor of the kitchen was constructed of wooden boards of various widths, stone, or especially in the South, brick. The walls were usually wood paneled or rough plastered or a combination of paneling and plaster. These early American kitchens were a far cry from the sanitary sheen of the white and chrome crispness of the kitchens of

The Eighteenth-Century Kitchen

the first three decades of the twentieth century. Hanging from the exposed hand-hewn beams or from long poles nailed to the ceiling were all manner of herbs, peppers, and dried rings of pumpkins and slices of apples. The apples and pumpkins were strung on sturdy linen thread.

The back-bars inside the vast fireplaces were mostly of iron in place of the seventeenth-century lug-pole, or back-bar, made of easily charred wood. The newly invented swinging crane was a convenient addition to or replacement for the back-bar, making the cook's job of pot hanging and tending safer and cooler over the ample fire. Trammels were pothooks made of two sections. The most common type consisted of a flat bar with a series of holes into which the second bar hooked. The pot could then be raised or lowered by changing the position of the bottom hook. Another type of

The kitchen of the Governor's Palace. *From Colonial Williamsburg*

trammel was the sawtooth, or ratchet, trammel in which one bar had notches to hold the second bar. Ornate trammels were made in variations of these types.

The burdensome utensils hanging from the multitude of trammels and pothooks consisted of primitive pots, different-sized kettles, and cauldrons made of brass, copper, or iron. It took a robust cook to lug the precious iron pot which sometimes weighed as much as forty pounds empty and considerably more when brimming with a hearty stew. The huge and costly kettles were passed down from generation to generation and were highly valued. The three-footed kettles with bail handles are often called gypsy kettles today. Other iron utensils included three-legged Dutch ovens with a deep lid

Brick Ovens: Colonial-costumed bakers mix their dough and add yeast and liquid just as their eighteenth-century predecessors did in the Raleigh Tavern Bake Shop in Williamsburg. The brick ovens are fired by wood, which is then cleared out when the proper temperature has been reached. The bread, cookies, and gingerbread-men made here are lifted into the ovens on long-handled peels. With the doors shut, the ovens hold baking temperature for hours. *From Colonial Williamsburg*

Wrought-iron
Pennsylvania German
eighteenth-century double
trammel. *Courtesy
Philadelphia Museum
of Art*

on which hot coals were placed, trivets, and basket-like vegetable boilers with short legs to fit into the various pots.

Skewers were an important kitchen accessory in the eighteenth century, every kitchen having a set of six or more hand-wrought iron ones hanging on a plain or fancy skewer rack. The skewers were of varying lengths to suit every need. Iron wafer and waffle irons had oval, round, or square heads and simple-to-elaborate grid designs. Their handles were often three feet long to keep from baking the cook as well as the wafer. Long handles were also used on the swivel toasters and the broilers. The broilers were round or oblong and the nicer ones were constructed so as to rotate.

Hand-wrought triangular trivets were useful fireplace adjuncts and came with long or short legs to vary their distance from the hot fireplace coals. Iron salamanders, long-handled utensils with flat, disc-shaped heads, were heated red hot and waved over cookies, pastry, and roasts to brown them. They were probably named for the mythical salamander believed to be able to endure fire without harm. Iron forks and ladles were of many shapes and sizes; for example, toasting forks had broad and widely spaced tines to hold food more securely. Skillets with three legs and long handles for cooking over the embers, picturesquely called "spiders," ranged from very small to extra large in capacity. Hanging iron Betty lamps burned grease and oil and were used in place of or in addition to candles. Steel-yard scales were often hung by the fireplace, and the mantel usually held a sadiron or two.

An easel-like triangular-shaped trivet with a wooden handle kept a plate or two warm near the fire for the later serving of food. A large wooden rack over the fireplace held the iron spit rods of many lengths for use on the andirons. Adjustable or stationary brackets on the hand-wrought andirons held the spit on which the roasting meat was secured. Some old spits had prongs to hold the meat more securely. Basket spits, which looked like cages, held game birds and small pieces of meat for roasting. Bird spits with a frame and hooks for hanging birds had a drip pan beneath and set on their own four legs close to the fire.

Copper and brass were used for many kitchen utensils. Besides the kettles and pots there were skimmers, ladles, spoons, pastry jaggers, bedwarmers with pierced covers and long handles of wood or iron, funnels, hanging salt boxes, large bowls, and colanders. The most luxurious pieces of copper were the elaborately shaped food molds of lovely design. The brightly reflecting surfaces of these items added to the cheerful glow of the almost constant fire.

The Raleigh Tavern kitchen served the Raleigh Tavern, the most famous of Williamsburg hostelries, during the eighteenth century. The kitchen building also houses the original baking room of the Raleigh Tavern, today an operating Craft Shop.
From Colonial Williamsburg

As a result of careful reconstruction, the kitchen of the George Wythe House looks much the way it did during colonial days. The furnishings are those of an eighteenth-century kitchen. A collection of brass and iron skimmers, strainers, and ladles hang at either side of the fireplace. The large built-in oven is used in baking. The tin oven in front of the fireplace is for roasting meats. An early biscuit block stands against the left wall. Attendants in authentic costume are on hand in the kitchen to explain its furnishings to visitors. *From Colonial Williamsburg*

There were few items of tin. The tin push-up, so called "hog-scraper," candlestick was common. This candleholder had a round base with a sharp edge. Clever farmers grasped the candlestick by its shaft and used this sharp edge to scrape the bristles from hogs at butchering time. The edge could be resharpened as necessary. This form of candlestick was the most commonly used during the eighteenth and nineteenth centuries. Many models had ejectors for removing the candle stub; others had a sharp projecting hook on their top rim which could be stuck into the wall, a beam, or the mantel or hooked over the back of a chair; some had both additional features. The tin lantern, which now erroneously bears the name of the famous patriot Paul Revere, was also a kitchen favorite. The one which commonly bears Revere's name is a round, pierced-tin lantern, whereas the type he carried was actually a square, glass-sided one. The old, large, tin graters looked much like their modern-day counterparts. There were tin coffee-bean roasters, the common boxlike type and a cylindrical type which was twirled on its iron point in the fireplace to assure more even roasting of the beans. The pride of a few kitchens was a tin reflecting oven, a half-round tin container about two feet in length with a spit and skewers inside. Its open side was placed facing the fire in the fireplace, and the tin front retained and reflected the heat. It was sometimes called a "tin kitchen," "kitchen" meaning "to cook." Tin candle boxes protected the expensive candles from marauding mice. And, of course, there were the tin candlemolds in which the candles were formed. A tin item made in the shape of a dustpan, but pierced with small holes, was a sandsifter used in the scouring of the iron pots and utensils.

Round and oval wooden boxes in graduated sizes held flour and spices, while hanging wooden boxes stored salt. Round, covered, wooden sugar bowls held the sugar after it was cut from its cone. In those days sugar came in loaves or cones wrapped in deep-blue paper. Sugar cutters or nippers (also called "sugar shears") were used to reduce it to pieces of a suitable size. Silver sugar tongs were used at the table to lift the lumps of sugar from their container to the teacup. These

Tin "hog-scraper" candlestick, eighteenth-century. *Courtesy National Gallery of Art*

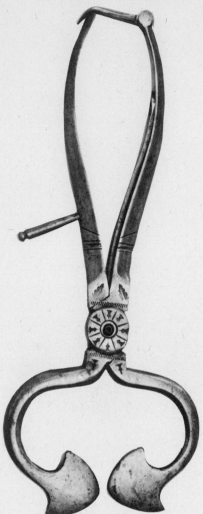

small tongs, with shell- or claw-shaped ends, were made in either flexible arch or scissorlike types. Wooden mortars and pestles, some of mammoth size, were used to pulverize spices and herbs. Wooden coffee grinders and smaller spice mills were common. The dustpan was usually of wood, too, and its companion broom was constructed of twigs bound to a stick. Sometimes a one-piece birch broom, made of a birch sapling with one end splintered and tied, was used. Wooden cookie boards were carved in fanciful designs.

Other materials found in the kitchen were pewter, for the many porringers and plates, and yellow pottery ware, for bowls and colanders. Home-grown gourds served as economical, ready-made dippers and ladles. Not quite kitchenware, but often found hanging in the old kitchens, were wooden ice skates with iron blades and iron pipe tongs with which embers from the fireplace were grasped for lighting the old clay and corncob pipes. A bellows and a fireplace shovel were indispensable.

The eighteenth-century kitchen required a multitude of kitchenware, and today, as then, these kitchens possess a quaint, warm charm which make them cozy and inviting.

Steel sugar nippers, eighteenth-century. *Courtesy Henry Francis du Pont Winterthur Museum*

Silver sugar tongs, circa 1800. *Courtesy National Gallery of Art*

The Victorian Kitchen

The Victorian kitchen was a bright, warm, and cozy room with a pleasant window or two, plants on the windowsill, and an easy chair with a workbasket nearby for sewing, mending, and darning materials. The curtains were of gaily printed chintz or of economical white muslin. Pots of flowers or a little crop of parsley, mint, or other herb thrived by the light of the windows. A general air of comfort pervaded the whole room.

The walls were painted or calcimined a bright hue, salad green being a favorite color. The woodwork was painted or fancifully grained. The kitchen walls were sometimes covered with a high wainscot painted a soft dove-gray, a tint that wore well and cleaned easily.

The floors were plain narrow strips of wood, painted or stained. Linoleum was sometimes used and made a floor covering both gayer and easier to clean than a wooden floor. Another type of floor covering, called "lignum," was composed largely of cork fiber; and another, called "lignotec," was made of wood fiber.

Nineteenth-century kitchen in Abraham Lincoln's home in Springfield, Illinois. *Courtesy Lincoln's Home State Memorial*

Tin pie lifter with
wooden handle for
use in coal stove

The Richmond Range.

Scores of Thousands of
Families testify to their
Superiority for

RICHMOND

Capacity,
Convenience,
Comfort.

THE BEST.

Send for Circular to
RICHMOND STOVE CO. Norwich, Conn.

*From Century
Magazine, Aug. 1887*

The kitchen sink was of iron, soapstone, wood, granite, or crockery, depending upon the means and preferences of the housekeeper. The stove burned hard or soft coal, wood, or cobs; it cooked the food, heated the water, and boiled the laundry. In the winter the stove heated the room to a cozy warmth; in the summer it made the room uncomfortably hot.

The kitchen table was wood, plain or painted. Sometimes a piece of linoleum matching that on the floor was shaped into a durable table cover. A length of oilcloth was a common table covering. Small rag rugs made a comfortable spot for the cook or dishwasher to stand by the stove and sink. Cheap woven rag rugs were sold by door-to-door

Cont'd on page 30

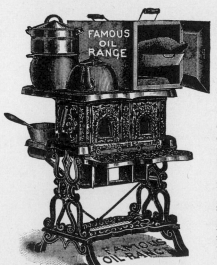

FAMOUS
OIL
RANGE

Ideal Summer Cooking.

A VOID the heat of a coal stove, by using the **Famous Oil Range** with Four Powerful Burners. Superior to any Coal, Gas or Gasoline stove. The only oil cooking apparatus made that is **Efficient, Durable** and **Safe.** Will do all the Cooking, Washing and Ironing of the Family. Uses the Regular Stove Furniture. Has Seamless Lead Tank. **Is Non-explosive** and **Odorless.** Has **Curved Burners** on the principle of the Rochester or Student Lamp, making it one-third more powerful than any other stove of equal size. Is indorsed by the leading housekeepers of the country.

Write us for Full Descriptive Circulars and name of the nearest agent. Either of the manufacturers whose names are given below can put you in the way of getting one of these stoves at a reasonable price.

Smith & Anthony Stove Co., - - Boston, Mass.
Brand Stove Co., - - - - Milwaukee, Wis.
Leibrandt & McDowell Stove Co., Philadelphia, Pa.
Manufacturers of the Famous Oil Range.
See advertisement in March and April "Century."

*From Century
Magazine, May 1889*

DIGHTON FURNACE COMPANY,

MANUFACTURERS OF

Wrought Iron Pipe,

FOR STEAM, WATER, AND GAS.

EVERY FOOT OF PIPE PROVED BY HYDRAULIC PRESSURE,
AND WARRANTED SOUND.

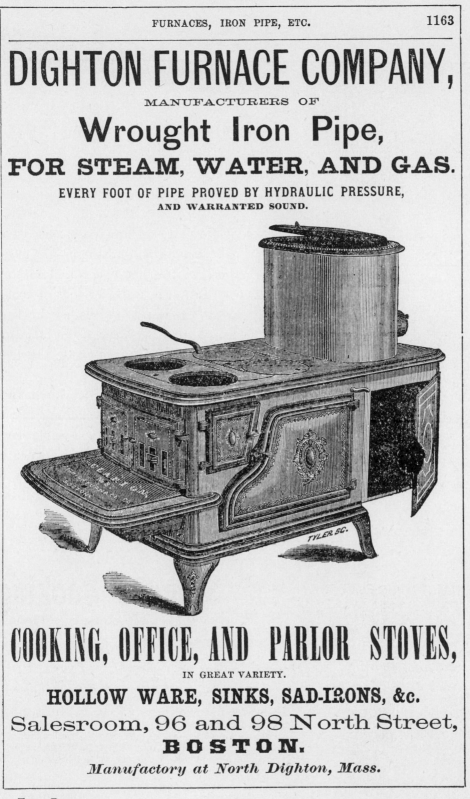

COOKING, OFFICE, AND PARLOR STOVES,

IN GREAT VARIETY.

HOLLOW WARE, SINKS, SAD-IRONS, &c.

Salesroom, 96 and 98 North Street,

BOSTON.

Manufactory at North Dighton, Mass.

*From Boston
Directory, 1869*

From Munsey's Magazine,
Mar. 1898

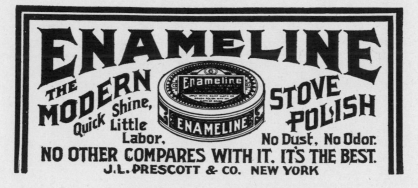
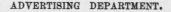
From Munsey's
Magazine, Mar. 1898

From Boston
Directory, 1869

*From Boston
Directory, 1869*

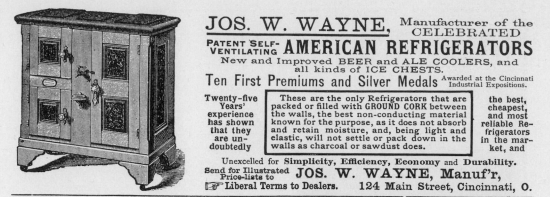

From Century Magazine, May 1888

JEWETT'S REFRIGERATORS

From Century Magazine, May 1889

From Harper's Bazaar, July 15, 1887

From Harper's, Mar. 1892

From Ladies' Home Journal, Aug. 1896

C. J. SIMONDS,

DEALER IN

New and Second-Hand Stoves,

**BRITANNIA, AND
GLASS WARE,**

Together with a general assortment of

First-Class Kitchen Furnishing Goods,

151 LEVERETT STREET, BOSTON.

Particular attention given to the Repairing of Tin Ware. Stoves put up with despatch.

*From Boston
Directory, 1869*

C. C. WOOD & CO.,

Tinsmiths, and Sheet Iron Workers,

ALSO, DEALERS IN

STOVES,

BRITANNIA,

And all kinds of TIN WARE,

KITCHEN FURNISHING GOODS,

KEROSENE LAMPS, &c.

Particular attention paid to all kinds of JOBBING in the line.

No. 33 Leverett Street,

BOSTON.

*From Boston
Directory, 1869*

SEND US $1.00 AND THIS AD. and we will send you this BIG 410-pound new 1899 model nickel trimmed **ACME STEEL RESERVOIR RANGE** by freight, C. O. D., subject to examination. You can examine it at your freight depot and if you pronounce it the handsomest and most perfect range you ever saw and equal to ranges that retail at $50.00 **OUR SPECIAL PRICE, $28.55,** less the $1.00 sent with order, or to $60.00, pay the freight agent **OUR SPECIAL PRICE, $28.55,** $27.55 and freight charges. The freight charges on this range will average $1.50 for 500 miles; greater or lesser distances in proportion.

WE GUARANTEE THIS THE HIGHEST GRADE STEEL RANGE ON THE MARKET, made from extra heavy Stanton refined sheet steel, 2-gauges thicker than is usually used, wrought steel connection construction throughout, wrought steel oven plate, braced and bolted, lined throughout with non-conducting fireproof asbestos, economizing fuel and making it the BEST BAKER MADE; has heavy duplex grate for either hard or soft coal, or wood, extra large porcelain lined reservoir.

THIS ACME IS A 6-HOLE HIGH CLOSET RESERVOIR STEEL RANGE, 8-18 size; oven 18x19x12 inches; closet is 32½x14 inches; firebox, for wood, 20 inches. FINISH— Highly enameled with best locomotive black, striped in fine lines of bronze, richly nickel-plated and ornamented throughout, heavy nickel bands on balanced oven doors, nickel oven door ornament, heavy nickel bands full length of top, front and ends; large nickel towel rod, nickel bands on corners and bottom, all doors nickel plated, heavy nickel plated shield on reservoir, heavy nickel bands on high shelf and roll closet, nickel plated tea shelf, nickel plated pipe draft. No Handsomer or Better Range Made. **WE ISSUE A WRITTEN BINDING GUARANTEE** with every range and guarantee safe delivery to your railroad station. Your local dealer would ask $50.00 to $60.00 for such a range. **ORDER AT ONCE** and save $25.00. WE SELL STEEL RANGES from $16.95 up; COOK STOVES $4.90 and up; HEATERS $1.90 and up. **WRITE FOR FREE STOVE CATALOGUE.** Address **SEARS, ROEBUCK & CO. (Inc.), Chicago.**

In answering any advertisement on this page it is desirable that you mention MUNSEY'S MAGAZINE.

*From Munsey's
Magazine, Feb. 1899*

"Grand Andes" RANGE.

The Leading Range. Never fails to give perfect satisfaction. Sold by the leading dealers.

MANUFACTURED BY

PHILLIPS & CLARK STOVE CO.,

Geneva, N. Y.

From Harper's, Mar. 1892

The Best Preparation for Housekeeping is a

WIRE GAUZE DOOR

As used Exclusively in the New Hub Range.

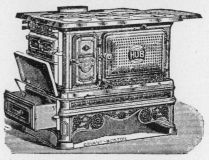

PERFECT COOKING

Is the most important item in the domestic economy. By using the Wire Gauze Oven Door with the new Hub Range, the skill of the cook is supplemented by the most perfect cooking apparatus ever made.

Three of the Hub Ranges with Wire Gauze Oven Doors are in constant use at the famous Boston Cooking-School, and are indorsed by them as being better than all others. Insist on your dealer giving you the new Hub Range. It is the very highest grade of cooking apparatus made, and when quality is considered is the lowest in price of any in the market. Over 100,000 Hub Ranges in use. The Hub line of goods are world renowned, and are sold by dealers everywhere. Special circulars sent on application.

SMITH & ANTHONY STOVE CO.

Manufacturers of Hub Stoves, Ranges and Furnaces,

52 & 54 Union St. Boston, Mass.

*From Century
Magazine, May 1888*

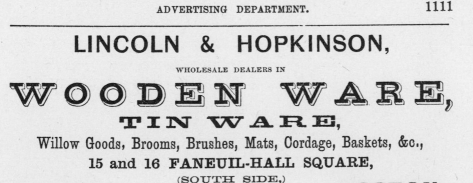

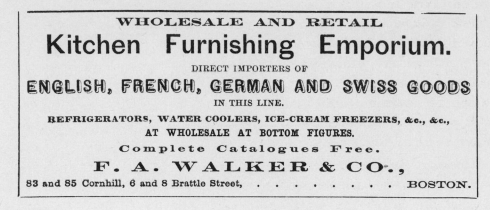

*From Boston
Directory, 1869*

salesmen. Women with the talent and the time braided their own rugs from remnants of clothing and household fabrics.

The Victorian pantry was a small room ranging in size from six feet by six feet to seven feet by fourteen feet. The pantry was provided with a table or a table-shelf that could be raised or lowered as necessary and shelves and drawers for storing supplies. These shelves were either open or concealed behind doors with solid wooden fronts or doors with curtained glass panels. The flour barrel and sugar bucket were also stored in the pantry. A round cover with a handle was used to close the flour barrel. The flour had to be protected from dust, insects, and dampness.

On the other side of the pantry there was often a row of hooks on the wall for aprons and towels. If there was no broom closet, and there usually was not, the carpet sweeper, broom, mop, carpet beater, pails, dust pans, and feather dusters were stored in the pantry. Oil and wicks for the oil lamps and a handy small stepladder were also usually kept here.

Upright and chest refrigerators were made of hardwood. Some boasted walls insulated with ground cork and shelves made of slate; others offered built-in water coolers. A few models were advertised as having sideboards and china closets to match. These refrigerators, often made of golden oak, are usually referred to as "iceboxes" today. The average family-sized ones held 90 to 100 pounds of ice. There were many manufacturers and numerous models from which to choose.

Cooking utensils were made of various materials. Cast-iron utensils were still popular, but in smaller sizes and lighter weights than previously employed. Smaller kettles of graniteware and of porcelain-lined cast iron were in general use. Tinware was still widely favored, and the seamless models were considered the best. For mixing cake and bread, large, yellow, earthenware bowls were preferred.

BOWLS.

	Rockingham.	Yellow.
No. 2..3 gals....	.....	$8.00 doz.
No. 3..2 gals....	.....	5.75 "
No. 4..1½ gals....	$4.50	4.25 "
No. 6..1 gals....	3.25	3.00 "
No. 9.. ½ gals....	2.25	2.00 "
No. 12..1½ qts.	1.60	1.50 "
No. 18..1 qt.......	1.25	1.10 "
No. 24..1½ pts.....	.75	.60 "
No. 30..1 pt......	.60	.50 "
No. 36.. ¾ pt......	.50	.40 "

NAPPIES.

	Rockingham.	Yellow.
6-inch ....$ .90		$ .80 per doz.
7-inch 1.10		1.00 "
8-inch 1 35		1.20 "
9-inch 1.65		1.50 "
10-inch 2.10		1.90 "
11-inch 2.65		2.40 "
12-inch 3.25		3.00 "

PIE PLATES.

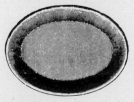

	Rockingham.	Yellow.
7-inch..............$ .75		$ .65 per dozen
8-inch.............. .85		.75 "
9-inch.............. .95		.85 "
10-inch.............. 1.05		.95 "

From Syracuse Stoneware Co. broadside of Aug. 15, 1896

MUGS.

	Rockingham.	Yellow.
No. 24....1 pint.....................$ .85		$ .75 per doz.
No. 30.... ¾ pint..................... .75		.65 "
No. 36.... ½ pint..................... .65		.55 "

The Early Twentieth- Century Kitchen

Cleanliness and orderliness were the rules of the early twentieth-century kitchen. Everything about the kitchen—floor, walls, ceiling, and furnishings—was wont to be practical, convenient, orderly, and above all, clean.

A wide variety of durable materials was available for the kitchen floor—large red clay quarry tiles, small white octagonal ceramic tiles, concrete, and granolith (an artificial stone of granite cement). Pine and hardwood floors were acceptable, for their inexpensiveness if for no other reason. These wooden floors were kept scrupulously clean by scrubbing and were sometimes waxed. Linoleum in single colors or patterns was considered an excellent floor covering; it deadened sound, and its flexibility was easy on the feet. Heavy oilcloth was sometimes used with satisfactory results in place of the more expensive linoleum. Occasionally the whole floor was covered with cork. Even when other coverings were used, it was suggested that comfortable, resilient cork mats be placed for the cook to stand upon before the table, sink, and range.

Glazed white ceramic tiles commonly covered the entire walls or at least the wainscot. Glossy enamel paint was recommended for above the wainscot or for the whole walls if tile was not used. The ceilings were also painted with gloss enamel so that all could be scrubbed from time to time. The enamel outlasted a flat paint and resisted the absorption of steam created by cooking and ironing. Wallpaper, unless glazed, was considered unhygienic for kitchen walls. White paint was chosen to complete the sanitary look, although sometimes black enamel was used to paint around the work areas if they were not tiled. The snowy purity of the white paint demanded the very acme

of cleanliness and neatness. The all-white kitchens just had to be kept scrupulously clean.

Sometimes both coal stoves and gas ranges were used in the same kitchen, the gas ranges being cooler for cooking in the summer months. Combination coal-gas ranges were available but were not as commonly used. These combination ranges burned natural or fuel gas and coal or wood. Electric ranges were expensive, but required less labor than the gas or coal stoves. Ventilating hoods were favored for carrying off steam and cooking odors. Gas or electric fixtures provided the necessary artificial lighting. Sinks were usually made of "white ware," an early twentieth-century name for solid porcelain or white porcelain-enameled iron sinks, or occasionally of soapstone rimmed with rubber

From Building with Assurance, Morgan Woodwork Organization, 1921

MIZEN

"I Can Always Depend on My Automatic Cook"

"I like the kind of cooking it does, and the reasonable cost, too, but the best thing about my Westinghouse Automatic is the fact that I don't have to stand over it every minute. I know that I needn't stay and watch it; my dinner will be ready when I get home."

SPOILED FOOD is a total loss. Whether ruined by too much heat, or by too little, food that is not properly cooked represents waste in good material and fuel as well as in time. Modern practice in the kitchen seeks to eliminate all these, by means of cooking methods that are independent of variations and shortages in the supply of available fuel.

Fuel shortages cause no problem in the kitchen that is equipped with the Westinghouse Automatic Electric Range. It provides even heat that never varies with the season or the time of the day. Winter and summer, morning, noon or night, it is a range that a woman can trust.

WESTINGHOUSE ELECTRIC & MANUFACTURING CO.

Convenience outlets in base boards and walls enable you to make the fullest use of Westinghouse appliances for the home. They include "the Iron that Women Designed", the Cozy Glow Heater, the Percolator, the Turnover Toaster, and the Toaster Stove. Your light and power company, or the Westinghouse Store, will give you the facts, gladly.

★

Westinghouse
ELECTRIC RANGES WITH AUTOMATIC CONTROL

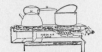

The Super Vulcan Burner produces hottest, steadiest gas flame known.

Each burner produces 4 different zones of heat—all at the one time.

And Smoothtop's oven has a truly dependable heat-regulator.

NEW COOKERY METHODS COOKERY RESULTS

Think of a gas range whose top is flat, and whose burners are enclosed underneath this solid top!

Think of being able to cook four vessels over a single burner!

Think of getting 4 zones of ideal cooking heat from each burner!

Think of these things—and you realize at once how startlingly new—how revolutionary—is the new Smoothtop Gas Range.

Domestic Economists hail the new Smoothtop as the creator of an entirely new cookery, easier, better. Whole meals can be kept simmering for hours without danger of drying out or burning. Each Super Vulcan Burner has an aeration plate and provides 4 distinct heats—one for speed boiling, one for gentle boiling, one for simmering and one for warming. All at the same time! And Smoothtop's oven has been lowered from the unhandy position top-stove to convenient, table-drawer level...Teachers and Students of Domestic Economy are especially invited to visit their local Gas Companies and see Smoothtop demonstrated.

Smoothtop
REG. US PAT OFF
GAS RANGE
WITH SUPER VULCAN BURNERS

Brass teakettle whistle to
insert in spout, patented
1923

KITCHEN CLOCK

A kitchen clock that looks so good you can hang it in
the dining room. Every woman who has seen this
clock has bought one. The face of the clock is a 9½-
inch white dinner plate with black hands and figures;
the Dutch design in blue varies somewhat in character.
A wonderful imported 8-day clock. Keeps perfect
time. Can be regulated by shortening or lengthening
the pendulum. Sent prepaid to any present subscriber
for sending seven (7) new subscriptions at $1.50 each,
or Cash Price, $5.25.

*From American
Cookery, 1925*

braid to reduce clatter and breakage. If two sinks
were used, as was sometimes the case, one for pots
and pans was of soapstone and one for dishes and
silverware was of gray or white enameled iron.

The worktable was of plain wood or had a zinc-
covered or an enameled top. A marble-topped table
for making pastry was a useful addition to the
kitchen if space and finances permitted.

Free-standing or built-in kitchen cupboards
held supplies, pots and pans, and dishes. Most
had wooden doors, but some had glass-paned,
hinged doors or doors which lifted up and slid
back like those of some old-fashioned bookcases.

Pots and pans were made of graniteware, aluminum, tin, cast iron, copper, or brass. The difficulty of keeping the last two metals clean and
their expensiveness made them the least commonly used materials. Aluminum was gaining in
popularity.

A reliable clock on a special clock shelf or a
key-wound, eight-day hanging clock were useful
kitchen accessories. Coffee, tea, salt, and spices
were stored in canisters decorated in the Bavarian
peasant style. Simple rod-pocket curtains were
made of scrim—a light, coarse, cotton or linen
fabric.

In the homes of the well-to-do, a laundry room
was adjacent to the kitchen and contained such
modern appliances as an electric mangle and an
electric drying oven. Gas-heated flatirons were a
new convenience. Electric irons, time and fuel
savers, assured a cooler kitchen or laundry room;
however, despite their saving and lightening labor,
they were not considered essential. The flatiron,
or sadiron, was still the favored ironing implement.

The new electric appliances, such as toasters,
coffeepots, and waffle irons, were light and portable and could be used in the kitchen or at the
breakfast table.

Iceboxes were still being used; some were built-in. A good one could be purchased for as little as thirty dollars, depending on the size, style, and lining.

During this period the kitchens were often heated by radiators, upon which an ingenious cook might place the dishes and serving plates to warm or the damp dish towels to dry.

It was suggested by house designers of the period that the kitchen be no larger than absolutely necessary. Otherwise an extra maid might be needed to keep it clean and in proper order!

From Woman's Home Companion, June 1918

Apple Parers and Cherry Stoners

During the eighteenth and early nineteenth centuries apples were a mainstay of the American diet. Apple trees were easily grown; and dried slices of apples kept well all winter long. The apples were pared, cored, cut into slices, and strung on strong linen threads, then hung to dry in the air. Another way apples were dried was to place the slices of apples on drying racks made of thin wooden strips or in shallow splint baskets. These were hung by iron hooks from the ceiling near the fireplace.

The earliest apple parers were made entirely of wood except for the blade and prongs. They either set on the table or were so constructed as to be screwed onto the table; a few were floor-standing bench models on their own legs. One looked much like a spinning wheel and was made of walnut. Most of these wooden parers were hand-crafted in the eighteenth and nineteenth centuries.

In the mid-nineteenth century the wooden parer was displaced by the iron parer. A picture drawn by the famous American artist, Winslow Homer, for the December 24, 1859, issue of *Harper's Weekly* was entitled "Fall Games—The Apple Bee." It showed a young man working what was probably one of the first factory-made, iron apple parers. The apple bee, like the quilting and sewing bees, was a favorite way of making fun out of tedious work. Some of these patented cast-iron apple parers not only pared the apple but cored it as well. More complex ones, such as the Vermont Apple Parer and the Hudson Parer, pared, cored, and sliced the apples. Special left-handed models were manufactured during the 1890s.

A simple tin apple corer was designed in the late 1800s. This unsophisticated tool was a hollow tin cylinder which was pushed into the apple

Walnut and steel apple parer, circa 1850. *Courtesy Colonial Williamsburg*

Wooden apple parer, nineteenth-century. *Courtesy National Gallery of Art*

Apple Corer.
5 and 10 cts.

around the core and withdrew the core as it was pulled out. Since one company which made this plain gadget marked it with their company name, "Fries," some people mistakenly think it is some sort of French-fry cutter.

The famous eighteenth-century London silversmith, Hester Bateman, designed a silver apple corer with an ivory handle for table use. Its blade was shaped like the simple tin kitchen corers, but it was, of course, much more elegant.

Cherry stoners, as the name implies, removed the seeds from cherries. Some of these worked by the action of a spring-driven extracting knife and removed the seed without crushing the fruit or the loss of juice. These machines worked on all sizes of cherries and seeded from twenty to thirty quarts in one hour. The Rollman Manufacturing Company of Mt. Joy, Pennsylvania, patented their spring-driven model in 1901. This model was designed to be clamped onto a table.

Crank-handled cherry stoners were made in table models with legs and in clamp-on types. Some of the table models had holes pre-formed in the legs to allow for screwing them securely to a table or a board for a more steady action. One table model came enameled, appropriately, cherry red. The crank-handled clamp-on-the-table models

Tin apple corer, wooden knob handle, nineteenth-century

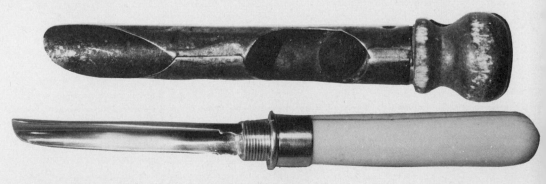

Silver apple corer with ivory handle, designed by Hester Bateman in London, circa 1774. *Courtesy The Art Institute of Chicago*

"ENTERPRISE"
CHERRY STONERS

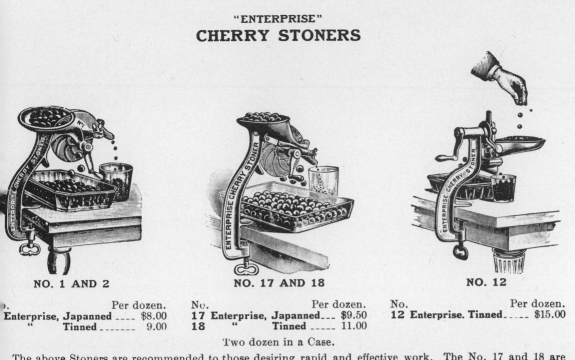

NO. 1 AND 2

NO. 17 AND 18

NO. 12

.	Per dozen.	No.		Per dozen.	No.		Per dozen.
Enterprise, Japanned	$8.00	**17**	Enterprise, Japanned	$9.50	**12**	Enterprise. Tinned	$15.00
" Tinned	9.00	**18**	" Tinned	11.00			

Two dozen in a Case.

The above Stoners are recommended to those desiring rapid and effective work. The No. 17 and 18 are constructed with a new Patented Regulating Device, the simplicity of which makes it easier to adjust Machines for the different sizes of Cherries, and absolutely insures the Jaws, retaining their position when set. The No. 12 Stoner is intended to stone Cherries with the least possible cutting or disfiguring.

From Biddle Hardware Co. Catalog, 1910

Cast-iron apple parer, nineteenth-century

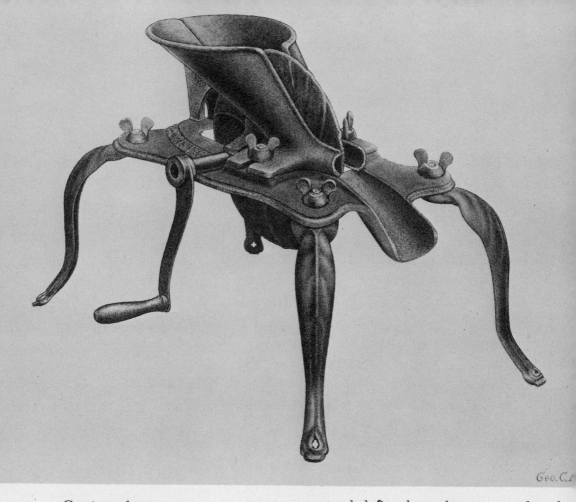

Geo. C.

Cast-iron cherry stoner patented 1863. *Courtesy National Gallery of Art*

were recommended for those desiring rapid and effective work. Some of these had a newly patented regulating device. This device made it easier to adjust the machines for different sizes of cherries and insured that their jaws would retain their set position. All models were made of cast iron heavily tinned or japanned to prevent rusting. The table models with legs were usually somewhat cheaper than the clamp-on types.

Dried apples, mincemeat, applesauce, apple butter, and apple pie required the paring of bushels of apples. Many pitted cherries were preserved, dried, eaten as a dessert fruit, and used in the making of cherry pies. Therefore, such gadgets as apple parers and corers and cherry stoners were welcome kitchen accessories.

In this day of comfortable central heating, one has difficulty imagining the need for a bedwarmer. However, bedwarmers were almost essential in the days when the fireplace was the sole source of heat. If, on a very cold day, you have ever been in a room heated only by a fireplace, you know that with even a roaring fire the room is quite cold just a few feet from it.

The old bedwarmers, some of which date back to Elizabethan England, were long-handled round pans of iron, copper, brass, or, rarely, pewter, with hinged, perforated covers. Some iron pans had copper or brass lids. The lids were usually decoratively engraved and punched. Iron-handled bedwarmers are considered to be older than the wooden-handled ones. Some of the wooden handles, of pine or maple, were decorated with stenciling. These "warming-pans," as they were also called, were kept hanging next to the fireplace. When needed, the pans were filled with hot coals and passed rapidly under the cold bed covers. Since the pans were quite heavy when filled with coals it took a strong arm to keep the pan moving and to prevent the scorching of the bed linen.

The earliest box-shaped footwarmers were constructed of all wood or all tin. Curly maple with a punched design made an especially attractive

Bedwarmers and Footwarmers

Brass bedwarmer with long wooden handle. *Courtesy Henry Francis du Pont Winterthur Museum*

Soapstone footwarmer
with tin carrying case.
*Courtesy Shelburne
Museum, Inc.; staff
photographer
Einars J. Mengis*

portable stove. In later designs wooden frames were fitted with perforated tin or zinc sides. The wood most commonly used was oak. Iron pans filled with glowing coals or hot bricks were set inside to provide the heat. These framed foot stoves were most commonly made in square shapes, but rare round and oval ones may be found. The square ones were sometime made in double and triple sizes to be shared by two or three people. They were carried to the stoveless churches and meetinghouses of the eighteenth century.

Copper and brass hot-water bottles were made in the 1800s. These were manufactured in an oval or a round shape with brass screw caps and carrying rings. Hollow, tin, U-shaped warmers were filled with boiling water and were used in

Soapstone bootwarmer. *Courtesy Shelburne Museum, Inc.; staff photographer Einars J. Mengis*

Soapstone footwarmer with bail handle. *Courtesy Shelburne Museum, Inc.; staff photographer Einars J. Mengis*

Bennington footwarmers, bottom two shaped to fit feet. *Courtesy Bennington Pottery and Porcelain by Richard Carter Barret, Crown Publishers*

carriages and sleighs during the nineteenth century, giving comforting warmth around the feet. Log-shaped tin footwarmers with a pull-out drawer for hot charcoal were covered with thick carpeting to help retain the heat. These were also used under the robes in sleighs and sleds on trips and in homes before central heating.

Pottery footwarmers, bedwarmers, and hot-water bottles were made by the potteries in Bennington, Vermont, the Sherwood Brothers Company in Pennsylvania, and other potters. These were made in stoneware, both plain and slip decorated, in mottled brown Rockingham, and in the patented flint enamel streaked blue, green, or yellow. Some unusual Bennington warmers were made to conform to the shape of the feet. Bennington also made the more conventional plump, cylindrical warmers, with a flat side to prevent them from rolling, which were picturesquely called "blind pigs." As late as 1920 the Dorchester Pottery Works of Dorchester, Massachusetts, made this type of warmer, called "Patented Henderson Foot Warmer." This warmer made a cozy bed companion on cold winter nights, and was used in baby carriages and automobiles as well as in beds. Pottery juglike bottles marked "Hot

From Ladies' Home Journal, Dec. 1920

From Sherwood Brothers Company Catalog, Bristol Ware

HOT WATER BOTTLES WITH SCREW CORK

No. 46

For hospital or sick-room use. For helping to keep up temperature after operations, or for persons afflicted with cold feet. Will keep warm all night when filled with boiling water.

Size	Price
1-quart	Per dozen, $4.00
2 "	" " 6.00

Here's a Seamless Hot Water Bottle.

The
❖ Hardman. ❖

PATENTED JANUARY 4, 1898.

It is made in a Mould.

IS ENTIRELY
SEAMLESS,

consequently cannot
leak.

There are no strips
or patches to tear off.

The Handle is so
fastened as to be
independent of the
bottle, and cannot
come off.

It is a distinct
novelty,

entirely original

and the

ONLY PERFECT

HOT WATER BOTTLE

EVER MADE,

being entirely without
seams, and made of
the very best quality
of materials.

It is one of the
most beautiful ex-
amples of artistic
moulded rubber work
ever produced.

GUARANTEED PERFECT.

THE RIVERSIDE RUBBER COMPANY,
BELLEVILLE, N. J., U. S. A.

From Shepp's Photographs of the World, 1891

Water" were purported to keep warm all night when filled with boiling water. These were most useful for persons afflicted with cold feet and for hospitals and sickrooms.

Soapstone footwarmers, handwarmers, and boot-warmers are described in the chapter "Soapstone."

The cork was king as a bottle stopper until the screw-cap was invented in 1858 by John Landis Mason and the metal crown seal in 1892 by William Painter. The corkscrew probably originated in about the sixteenth century. Elaborate corkscrews with scroll and animal-shaped handles were made in the seventeenth and eighteenth centuries in Europe, usually with protective sheaths which fitted over the working end. Elegant ones of sterling, pewter, brass, mother-of-pearl, or ivory were made in eighteenth-century America. At this same time more practical ones of iron and brass were also produced. Some of these folded for safety and convenience.

The mechanical type of corkscrew was a Victorian innovation. There were ratchet handles, "butterfly" screws, and the "folding-gate" type such as was patented by Weirs in 1884. The inexpensive wire corkscrew was a result of the ingenuity of William Rockwell Clough in the early 1870s. These simple little gadgets, already imbedded in the cork, were widely used on perfume

Bottle
and
Can Openers

Left: Brass stork corkscrew. *Right:* Nineteenth-century cast-iron corkscrew

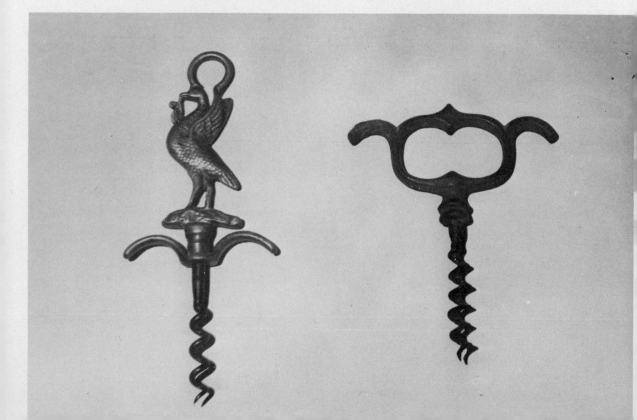

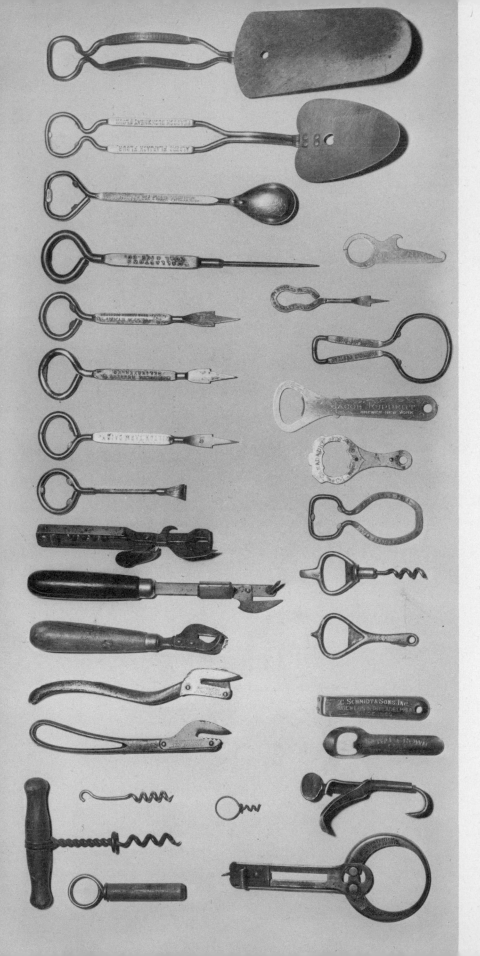

Assorted openers. *Photo by Willafred*

and medicine bottles, and were made by the millions.

The early 1900s brought a variety of early cap-lifter-type bottle openers for removing the new crown seal. These often bore the advertisements of flour-makers, soft-drink manufacturers, brewers, dairies, grocers, hotels, pharmacies, and even paint and hardware stores. These came with a diversity of ends opposite the bottle opener—ice-pick ends, pick ends for lifting the old cardboard milk-bottle closures, and ends for opening paint cans. Some had spoon ends, button-hook ends, and ends in the form of spatulas, pancake turners, potato mashers, and skimmers.

Patent-dated can openers are of particular interest because they can be placed in time. The iron

GREELY'S CORK EXTRACTOR.

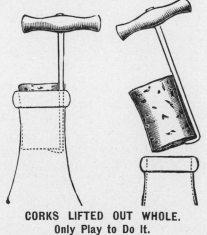

CORKS LIFTED OUT WHOLE.
Only Play to Do It.

The blade of the Extractor is inserted between the cork and the neck of the bottle.
The groove or air passage in the back of the blade comes against the glass, allowing the air to pass in as the cork is drawn, thereby preventing suction; hence the cork comes out easily and whole.

SOLD EVERYWHERE.

B. J. GREELY, Patentee,
715 WASHINGTON ST., BOSTON.

From Iron Age,
Jan. 9, 1890

CAN OPENERS

"I. X. L."

Iron Handle, Tempered Steel Blade.

"I. X. L." Nickel Plated............Per dozen .75

One dozen in a Box.

SPRAGUE PATTERN

Tempered Steel Blade.

No. **10** Iron Handle.............Per dozen .90
" **20** Wood " .... " " 1.00

One dozen in a Box.

"CROCODILE" BOTTLE CAP EXTRACTOR AND CAN OPENER

Tempered Steel.

"**Crocodile**," Nickel Plated...........Per dozen $1.20

One dozen in a Box.

"NONE SUCH" CAN OPENER AND CORKSCREW

Tempered Steel Blade.

"**None Such**," Nickel Plated.........Per dozen $1.50

One dozen in a Box.

PEERLESS "ANTI-SLIP" GRIPPER

Cutlery Steel Blade, Nickel Plated Japanned Handle.

"**Peerless**"........................ Per dozen $1.50

One dozen in a Display Box.

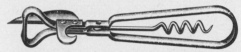

IMPROVED "KING" CAN AND BOTTLE OPENER

Cast Steel Oil Tempered Blades.

"**King**"........................Per dozen $1.50

One dozen in a Box.

"NEVER-SLIP," WOOD HANDLE

Cast Steel Blades, Oil Tempered.

No. **30½** Polished Hardwood Handle..Per doz. $1.70

One dozen in a Display Box.

"NEVER-SLIP," IRON HANDLE

Cast Steel Blades, Oil Tempered.

No. **30** Nickel Plated ....Per dozen $1.70

One dozen in a Display Box.

"PERFECT"

Adjusted to Cut Any Size Can. Cuts either Top off or out of Can. Requires no Sharpening. All Metallic and Cutting Parts made from Case Hardened Steel.

"**Perfect**" ....Per dozen $3.50

One dozen in a Box.

From Biddle Hardware Co. Catalog, 1910

CORK SCREWS

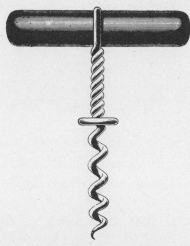

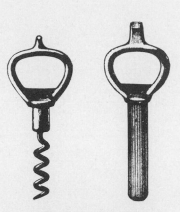

Half Size of No. 079.

Bessemer Steel Wire Cork Screw, with Wood Handle and Wooden Tube to Protect the Point of the Screw, Maple Handles, Assorted, Natural Finish and Ebonized.

No. **079** Tinned Screws _____ .90

One dozen on a Card.

Half Size of No. 04.

Bessemer Steel Combination Cork Screw, Crown and Seal Opener for the Pocket, with Wooden Tube, as illustrated above.

No. **04** Nickel Plated _ Per doz. $1.00

Two dozen on a Card.

NO. 06146

Norway Steel, Nickel Plated Screws, Maple Handles.

No. **06146** ___ Per dozen $1.50

Half dozen on a Card.

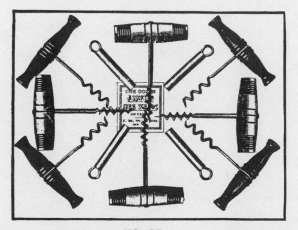

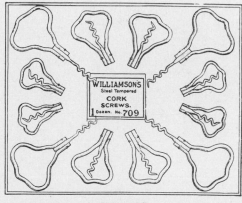

NO. 27

Cut Steel and Steel Wire, Assorted, Wood Handles, Stained Assorted Colors.

No. **27** Nickel Plated _____Per dozen $2.40

One dozen on a Card.

NO. 709

Extra Quality, Steel Tempered, Nickel Plated.

No. **709** Assorted Sizes _____Per dozen $2.40

One dozen on a Card.

From Biddle Hardware Co. Catalog, 1910

"Peerless" and "Delmonico" were patented in 1890, the "Never-slip" in 1892. The Star Can Opener Company of San Francisco, California, patented their thumbscrew can opener in 1920. Two multi-openers, the "King" and "None Such," were the predecessors of today's ordinary variety-store combined bottle, can, and cork opener. A thumb guard for this type opener was patented in 1929.

In the days of home canning, many openers were patented for use in loosening the screw lids of canning jars. J. C. Foster and Son of Pittsburgh, Pennsylvania, patented their "4 in 1" jar opener in 1910. The "Victory" was a jar opener that worked by a thumbscrew.

Old bottle, can, and jar openers came in a myriad of shapes and sizes. A varied collection of them may trace the development of canning and bottling through the years as man has sought better methods by which to preserve his foods.

Thousands of years ago, the ancient Egyptians baked bread in ovens and even bought bread from bakeries. Bread has been baked before the open fire and in ovens for many centuries.

The early settlers in America kneaded their dough by hand in deep, round, wooden-burl bowls or oblong bread troughs. The Pennsylvania Dutch, in particular, made their bread in dough boxes or dough trays, which were rectangular boxes with slanting sides and a lid. This lid could also be used as a kneading board. Some of these boxes, without legs, were made to place on the kitchen worktable, while others stood on their own legs. Some bread troughs were fitted with a long narrow rod to accommodate a temse or flour sifter. Large wooden spoons or paddles were used to mix the ingredients for the bread.

Before the brick bake oven next to the fireplace became a standard item, bread was slowly baked in a Dutch oven, a heavy iron pot-on-legs with a deep

Breadmaking Tools

Burl bowl made of bird's-eye maple, circa 1800. *Courtesy Colonial Williamsburg*

Early nineteenth-century scraper for dough board. *Courtesy The Metropolitan Museum of Art, gift of Mrs. J. Insley Blair, 1937*

lid on which hot coals could be placed. This method is supposed to have produced truly delicious bread and biscuits.

The preparation of the brick bake oven for the cooking of pies and bread was a long chore. First the oven was thoroughly heated with burning logs. Then the ashes were swept out, the chimney closed, the pies and bread put in, and the heavy iron door shut tight. Long, flat, paddlelike peels made of wood or iron were used to place and remove the loaves in the old fireplace ovens, loaves being put in pans or placed on layers of cabbage or oak leaves.

In the eighteenth century bread was often served on a bread board, a round or oblong board sometimes carved with religious sayings. In the late 1800s, it became fashionable to serve bread on glass bread platters. These, too, were bordered with such religious phrases as "Give us this day our daily bread."

"UNIVERSAL" BREAD MAKERS

NO. 2	NO. 44	NO. 4 AND 8
	The Top is on a Level with the Table. Can be used by a person sitting down.	Interior View, showing Kneader.

MADE OF HEAVY TIN AND SHEET STEEL

No. 2	"Universal,"	Small	Family	Size,	Capacity	2	Loaves,	Weight,	4¾	pounds		Per dozen	$16.20
" 44	"	Regular	"	"	"	2 to 6	"	"	7¼	"		" "	24.00
" 4	"	"	"	"	"	2 " 6	"	"	7¼	"		" "	24.00
" 8	"	Large	"	"	"	4 " 10	"	"	10½	"		" "	30.00

From Biddle Hardware Co. Catalog, 1910

The advent of the kitchen range simplified the baking of bread. It was a much easier task to fire a coal range than to heat the bake oven by the fireplace. The White House Bread Mixer and Kneader was awarded a Gold Medal at the St. Louis Exposition in 1904. This gadget, made by Landers, Frary, and Clark of New Britain, Connecticut, was a sort of tin bucket with cover which was clamped to the table. By turning its crank handle the bread ingredients inside were mixed and kneaded. A similar model made at a later date by the same company was marked "Universal Bread Maker." It is interesting to note that similar bread mixers are again being manufactured today.

Toward the end of the nineteenth century the tin bread-raiser came into use. This was a large tin bowl about fourteen inches in diameter with side handles and a rim base. It had a tight-fitting lid with a few perforations. Contemporary advertisements stated that it "makes dough light and spongy, prevents chilling." Interesting covered and fluted bread pans baked bread with corrugations to facilitate cutting even slices. These pans either clipped together or were held with wire loops at the ends. They were available in single- or double-loaf models. Efficient bread knives had open metal handles and sharp scalloped cutting edges.

BREAD BOARD.
$1.25.

BREAD KNIFE.
50 cts.

*From Van Heusen-
Charles Co. Catalog, 1898*

BREAD RAISERS.
Makes dough light and spongy, prevents chilling.
50 cts. to $1.25.

*From Van Heusen-
Charles Co. Catalog, 1898*

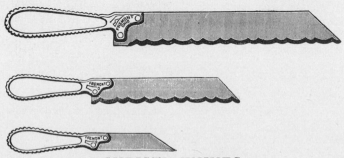

CHRISTY KNIVES.

3 in set.   Consisting of 1 Bread Knife; 1 Paring Knife; 1 Cake Knife.
65 cts. set.

*From Van Heusen-
Charles Co. Catalog, 1898*

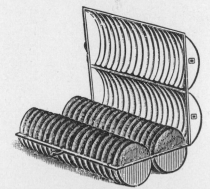

Covered and Fluted Crusty Bread Pans.

By using these Pans you have the very latest common sense way of baking a fine loaf of Bread.

Made in tin and sheet iron, 50 cts.

*From Van Heusen-
Charles Co. Catalog, 1898*

Brushes, Brooms, and Rug Beaters

The earliest brooms made in America were simply slender birch saplings with the ends splintered. First all the bark was removed from a sapling about six feet long and about two inches in diameter, then the wide end was splintered up about one foot, the hard core removed, and the splintered ends tied down tightly near the top with a length of hemp. About one foot two inches above this tied section, more flat slivers were cut down from the opposite direction, leaving about a two inch uncut ring between the two sets of splinters. The second bunch of splinters was folded over the first and bound securely. The rest of the sapling was shaped and smoothed to form a handle. These "Indian brooms," so-called because the technique for making them was learned from the Indian by the white man, were made at home or could be bought in the country store or from the itinerant peddler.

Tiny brooms similarly made were used for whisking eggs and whipping cream, slightly larger ones for cleaning pots and pans and for sweeping the ashes from the brick bake oven, and very large ones for heavy-duty sweeping such as a barn floor. More bristly brooms were made by cutting and binding only the first section of slivers.

In the eighteenth century broom-corn was grown for the specific purpose of broom manufacture, its branched panicles being easily made into brooms. Legend tells us that from a single seed which Benjamin Franklin took from a whisk of broom-corn in England have sprung all the broom-corn plants in this country.

The first brushes used by man were probably simple reeds. Later brushes and brooms were contrived of twigs or brushwood tied to a stick or a whittled handle. These, known since biblical

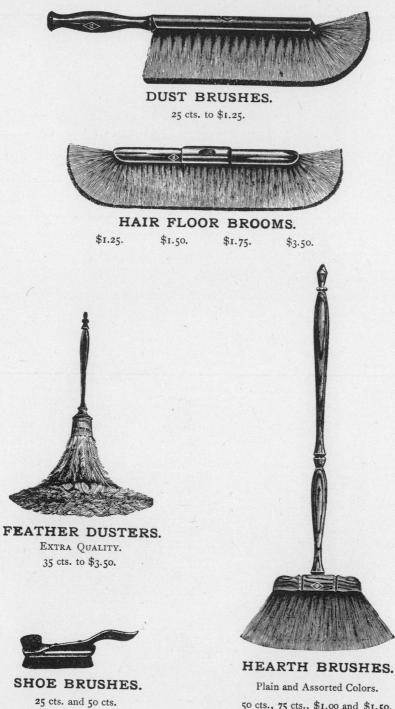

DUST BRUSHES.

25 cts. to $1.25.

HAIR FLOOR BROOMS.

$1.25. $1.50. $1.75. $3.50.

FEATHER DUSTERS.

EXTRA QUALITY.

35 cts. to $3.50.

SHOE BRUSHES.

25 cts. and 50 cts.

HEARTH BRUSHES.

Plain and Assorted Colors.

50 cts., 75 cts., $1.00 and $1.50.

From Van Heusen-Charles Co. Catalog, 1898

SILVER CREAM.

½ pint, 18 cts.
1 " 35 cts.

PUTZ CREAM.

Four sizes.

10 cts., 20 cts., 40 cts. and 75 cts.

FURNITURE POLISH.

25 cts.

The best we know of.

CYCLE POLISH.

25 cts.
Recommended very highly.

PUTZ POMADE.

For Cleaning Copper, Brass and Metal Goods.
5 and 10 cts.

STOVE POLISHING MITTEN AND DAUBER.

10 cts.

From Van Heusen-Charles Co. Catalog, 1898

times, were called "besoms." Heather or birch made a good besom. Many early American brushes were made from hog bristles. These stiff, coarse, glossy hairs made effective and durable brushes.

The Victorian era was the beginning of the fashion of a broom and a brush for every purpose. There were dust brooms, floor brooms, hearth brooms, whisk brooms, scrub brushes, crumb brushes, shoe brushes, clothes brushes, hat brushes, tooth brushes, shaving brushes, nail brushes, and brushes for cleaning the new-fangled water closets. Soft and springy goose feathers were made into feather dusters and into small brushes

From Biddle Hardware Co. Catalog, 1910

CARPET BEATERS

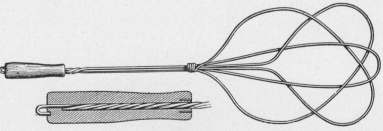

NO. 99

Made of No. 10 Steel Spring Wire, Covered with Coils, Retinned Head, Stained Handle.

No. **99 Niagara**, Length, 22 inches; Diameter of Head, 7½ inches _____Per dozen **$1.75**

One dozen in a Bundle.

NO. 13

Made of No. 13 Tinned Wire, 6 Wires in Head, 4 Wires in Shank, Handle will not come off.

No. **13** Length, 26 inches; Size of Head, 9 x 12 inches_____Per dozen **$1.75**

One dozen in a Bundle.

for buttering the crust of fresh bread to keep it soft. "Wing dusters," made from the wings of turkeys, geese, or chickens, were used as stove and hearth brushes. Housekeepers were warned not to leave these where the cat could chew them. However, they were also prone to destruction by moths and other insects.

Rug beaters were made from wire in many different patterns. Most had wooden handles and date from the Victorian era. Some all-wire ones were twisted into intricate shapes. An interesting wooden-handled one was marked "The Batwing Beater, Pat. Oct. 4, 1927, Johnson Novelty Co., Danville, Pa." It was one of the few bearing a patent date. Homemade wire beaters were formed by bending into a loop a piece of wire about nine feet long and attaching the ends to a broomstick. Rug beaters as well as furniture were also made of rattan, a popular material during the Victorian period. Flexible hickory switches were also used as rug beaters.

Cattle were brought to America soon after the Pilgrims settled here. Hence, butter may have been made by the settlers from the very earliest days of this country. However, since few butter churns were listed in seventeenth-century inventories, it is believed that little butter was made in the seventeenth century and that it did not become a really important dairy product until the eighteenth century. Prior to the mid-nineteenth century all butter was made at home, a task considered to be the work of the women and children. After the butter was churned, carrot juice was added to give it a rich, yellow color, and salt was added to improve the flavor.

The first churns were of the plunger type with a barrellike body of wooden staves held together by wooden hoops. In the nineteenth century the churning was made easier by the invention of the cylinder churn made of white cedar with a crank-type handle on the side, for it was easier on the arms to turn the crank handle than to lift and push a plunger. Other churns were worked by a pump-type arm or by a rocking motion. A tin churn, called a "piggy" churn because of its swinelike shape, was suspended from the ceiling by hooks and was swung back and forth. This model was made circa 1875. Churning the milk to butter was an arduous task no matter what type of motion accomplished the beating. Sometimes a dog on a tread mill was used to do the churning by attaching the mill to a churn.

After the butter was churned it was removed from the churn with a wooden scoop and placed in a bowl to be pressed with the hands or wooden butter paddles until the water was worked out of it. Wooden butter workers, which were wooden

Butter Churns, Molds, and Cutters

Poplar-wood butter
churn, circa 1855.
*Courtesy National
Gallery of Art*

boxes fitted with a corrugated wooden roller, were still sold for this purpose in the 1920s.

Next, the butter was packed into tubs or pressed into molds. The designs on the butter molds and butter stamps both decorated the butter and identified it as being the product of a certain farm or family. In later years, when the molds were factory-made on a wide scale with hundreds marked with the same design, this principle no longer applied. Butter molds were most commonly made of hardwood, but some were also made of glass, pottery, or aluminum. The wooden ones were usually round or rectangular; hexagonal or elliptical ones were more rare. Their designs were hand carved by the farmer himself or the most talented member of the family. Some factory-made ones had the designs pressed into the mold through a combination of steam and pressure; other commercially made ones were machine cut.

Molds that were subjected to hard usage, such as those used by hotels and restaurants, often had sturdy brass handles. An unusual type of mold produced a three-dimensional design rather than just a stamped motif, a rare mold of this type was wedge-shaped and held together by wooden pins. Animals were the favorite forms in this type of mold. The variety of designs on the stamps and molds included initials, stars, animals, flowers, fruit, sheaves of wheat, and numerous fanciful designs. The eagle, cow, sheep, deer, and swan are the most sought-after designs today. It is

*From F. A. Walker
& Co. Catalog, 1886*

No. 93 a. Butter Mould.   **No. 94 a.**   **No. 95 a.**

No. 94 a and No. 95 a.   New patterns of Wooden Butter Prints.
Every variety of Butter Prints for making Balls, Strawberries, Acorns, Wheat, Animals, etc.

HAND BUTTER PRINTS.

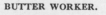

½ lb. Seeley Pattern, as shown in cut	$0.75
Baltimore Pattern	1.25
Round Print and Mould	.40

BUTTER WORKER.

Inside Measurement.	Cap.	Price
No. 1. 23c36x2½ in.,	50 lbs.	$15.25
No. 2. 20x36x2½ in.,	30 lbs.	13.25
No. 3. 17x27x2½ in.	20 lbs.	8.50

DANDELION BUTTER COLORING.

Dandelion Brand Butter Coloring is guaranteed to be purely vegetable, and that the use of same for coloring butter is permitted under all Food Laws—State and National.

Will not color the buttermilk; will never turn rancid; gives the brightest and best color; butter never becomes reddish; perfect economy in use. It is cheaper than any other coloring. Put up in four sizes.

Small size to color 500 lbs.	$0.35
Medium size to color 1250 lbs.	.65
Large size to color 2800 lbs.	1.25

CYLINDER CHURN—Illustrated.
CYLINDER CHURN.

Made of selected white cedar and well put up.
Full churning capacity.

No.	1	2	3	4
Gals.	1½	2	3½	6

Price, $4.25; 5.00; 6.00; 7.25.

BARREL CHURN.

Oak stave; steel top. it works by concussion and will not break the grain of the butter nor make it of a salvy consistency.

No.	0	1	2	3	4	5	6
Gallons churned	3	5	7	10	13	18	30
Price	$6.00	6.75	7.50	8.25	10.50	12.00	16.50

BUTTER SHIPPING BOXES.

36 ½-lb. prints	$15.50	20 lb. prints	$13.75
64 ½-lb. prints	17.60	30 lb. prints	16.00
80 ½-lb. prints	18.75	40 lb. prints	19.75
100 ½-lb. prints	23.25	56 lb. prints	23.75

From Mann's Seed Catalog, 1928

CHURNS

"MONUMENTAL" CHURNS

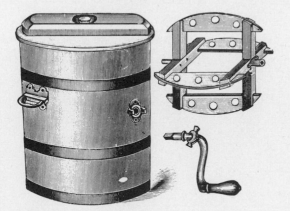

White Cedar. Galvanized Iron Hoops. Thumb-Screw Lock. Top Lifts Off. Finely Finished.

Capacity, quarts	8	12	20	30
"Monumental" Each	$2.25	2.50	3.00	3.50

IMPROVED CEDAR CYLINDER CHURNS

Double Dasher. Thumb-Screw Lock.
White Cedar. Galvanized Iron Hoops. The Crank is Locked to the Churn with a Clamp and Thumb Screw, which prevents Leakage.

No. 1 Capacity, 3 Gallons	Each	$2.50
" 2 " 4 "	"	3.00
" 3 " 7 "	"	3.50
" 4 " 10 "	"	4.00

From Biddle Hardware Co. Catalog, 1910

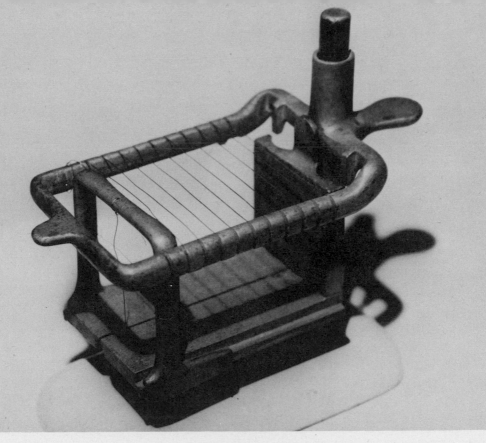

Elgin butter slicer for
restaurant use,
patented 1901

*From American
Cookery, 1925*

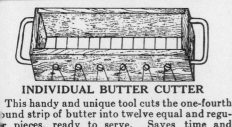

INDIVIDUAL BUTTER CUTTER
This handy and unique tool cuts the one-fourth
ⁿound strip of butter into twelve equal and regu-
r pieces, ready to serve. Saves time and
oney. Sent, postpaid, for one (1) new sub-
ription, or Cash Price, **75 cents.**

impossible to tell the age or origin of a mold by
its design or the shape of the mold since all
designs and all shapes were made continuously
from the end of the seventeenth century both
here and in Europe.

Glass molds were made, but proved impractical
on account of breakage, and pottery ones were
almost as fragile. Aluminum molds were sold by
Sears, Roebuck, and Company through its catalog
in the early 1900s, but they, too, never became
popular.

Grocers, hotels, and restaurants sometimes used
a gadget to slice a one-pound piece of butter into
four quarter-pound sections or into forty-eight
individual pats. This device was made of heavy
brass, nickel-plated and fitted with thin cutting
wires, with a base of speckled white-enameled
cast iron. It was manufactured by the Cleveland
Faucet Company in 1901. A simple series of wires

screwed to a wooden rectangle with metal end handles formed a butter cutter made during the beginning of the twentieth century. This handy kitchen tool cut the one-quarter-pound strip of butter into twelve equal and regular pieces, ready to serve.

Making butter was a tiring, time-consuming task, but the delicate flavor of the finished product made the chore worth while.

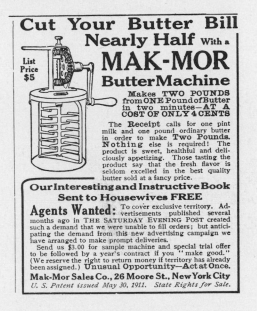

Cut Your Butter Bill Nearly Half With a **MAK-MOR ButterMachine**

List Price $5

Makes TWO POUNDS from ONE Pound of Butter in two minutes—AT A COST OF ONLY 4 CENTS

The Receipt calls for one pint milk and one pound ordinary butter in order to make Two Pounds. Nothing else is required! The product is sweet, healthful and deliciously appetizing. Those tasting the product say that the fresh flavor is seldom excelled in the best quality butter sold at a fancy price.

Our Interesting and Instructive Book Sent to Housewives FREE

Agents Wanted: To cover exclusive territory. Advertisements published several months ago in THE SATURDAY EVENING POST created such a demand that we were unable to fill orders; but anticipating the demand from this new advertising campaign we have arranged to make prompt deliveries.

Send us $3.00 for sample machine and special trial offer to be followed by a year's contract if you "make good." (We reserve the right to return money if territory has already been assigned.) Unusual Opportunity—Act at Once.

Mak-Mor Sales Co., 26 Moore St., New York City

U. S. Patent issued May 30, 1911. State Rights for Sale.

From Saturday Evening Post, Sept. 9, 1911

Choppers, Graters, and Cabbage Cutters

It would not be difficult to collect a hundred different old chopping knives. These handy food choppers, also called "mincing knives" or "mincers," were essential in the days of mince pies and homemade sausage that was made of chopped rather than ground meat.

Most of these choppers were handmade by the homesteader or made for him by the local blacksmith. Early all-iron ones with a curlicue end for hanging were primitive, but practical. Some had more comfortable wooden handles attached. The sizes and shapes of the choppers varied, and some had double blades. A rare one had the handle set at right angles to the blade rather than perpendicular to it. A novel one had a pivoting blade which could be rotated to three different cutting edges. Many wooden-handled choppers were factory-made in the nineteenth century. Those with a steel blade attached to an iron open handle were factory-made during the late nineteenth century and later.

One of the few choppers bearing a patent date was one marked "N. R. S. & CO., GROTON, N.Y. PATD. May 2 93, No. 40." It had a double, steel, X-shaped blade and a cast-iron open handle bearing the above information in raised letters.

From Iron Age,
Jan. 9, 1890

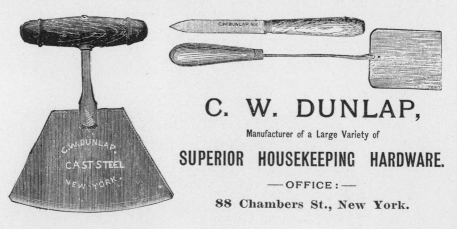

C. W. DUNLAP,

Manufacturer of a Large Variety of

SUPERIOR HOUSEKEEPING HARDWARE.

— OFFICE : —

88 Chambers St., New York.

68

Top left: Tin corrugated blade slicer. *Bottom left*: Factory-made chopper. *Right*: Triple-edged chopper, rotating blade

Hand-wrought iron chopping knife

MINCING KNIVES

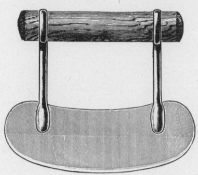

NO. 30 AND 03

No. **30**, Polished Steel Blades, Malleable Lip Shanks, Well Braced, Plain Natural Wood Handles.

Per dozen _____ .75

No. **03**, **Extra Large Blade**, same Style as No. 30, but with Black Enameled Handles.

Per dozen _____ .85

NO. 6

Extra Large, Polished Steel Blades, Two Steel Shanks encircling Handle, Polished Natural Wood Handles.

No. **6**_____Per dozen $1.50

NO. 5

Heavy Polished, Steel Blades, Fine Quality, Heavy Iron Handles, Well Enameled.

No. **5**_____Per dozen $1.80

NO. 7

Extra Quality, Hand Forged, Blades Tempered and Polished with Oil Finish, Black Enameled Handles.

No. **7**_____Per dozen $4.30

NO. 60 "DOUBLE ACTION"

Best Quality Steel, Nickel Plated Blades, Japanned Handles. The efficiency is double that of the ordinary Knives that only contact at a single point.

No. **60** "**Double Action**"_____Per dozen $4.00

All the above, one dozen in a Box.

From Biddle Hardware Co. Catalog, 1910

MINCING KNIVES

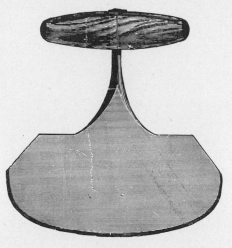

NO. 12

Extra Heavy Blade, Best Quality Cutlery Steel, Hand Forged, Finely Polished, Oil Finish, Tang Riveted through the Handle.

No. 12 ------------------------------Per dozen $5.00

One dozen in a Box.

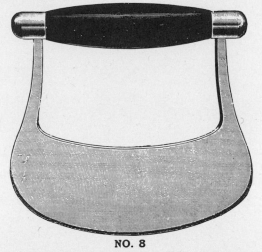

NO. 8

Extra Heavy Blade, Best Quality Cutlery Steel, Hand Forged, Finely Polished, Oil Finish, Enameled Handles with Oval End Nickeled Ferrules, Handles fastened with Pins through Tangs.

No. 8 -------------------------------Per dozen $5.50

One dozen in a Box.

NO. 400

Double Blade, Polished Steel, Steel Shank encircling the Handle, Plain Natural Wood Handles.

No. 400 ------------------------------Per dozen $1.00

One dozen in a Box.

NO. 06

Heavy Double Blade, Polished Steel, with Two Steel Shanks encircling Handle; Natural Wood Handles, Stained and Polished.

No. 06 ------------------------------Per dozen $2.30

Half dozen in a Box.

From Biddle Hardware Co. Catalog, 1910

Iron chopper patented
1893, one of few with
patent date

Conventional crank-handled food choppers or
grinders, devices with revolving wheels or teeth,
were used to cut, chop, or mince meats and vegetables. These simple machines were a great
convenience for the making of breakfast hash,
sausage meat, mincemeat, scrapple, chicken cro-
quettes, hamburg steak, and other dishes. The
Enterprise Meat and Food Chopper advertised
that it "Minces anything that can be minced."
The Great American Meat Cutters were available
in sizes from the "Family Size" to the "Hotel and
Boarding-house Size" to the "Butchers' Size." The
cost increased as the capacity increased. An 1890
price list quoted the Family Size at $2.75 and the
Butchers' Size at $8.00.

An assortment of old American graters would
include graters of various sizes and shapes and
for several purposes. The smallest kitchen graters
were the nutmeg graters, some of these being
intended to be carried in the pocket for flavoring
beverages when traveling or visiting. The Edgar
Nutmeg Grater was patented in 1891. In this
model the nutmeg was held in place by a spring

Left: Double-bladed
chopper. *Right:* Hand-
wrought chopper

DISSTON
ADJUSTABLE CROUT CUTTERS

This Cutter is very simple in construction, all the Knives can be adjusted to any cut by loosening Thumb Screws on sides, moving Slides backward or forward as required, one movement adjusting all the Knives alike.

1 Knife, with Box,	24x7 inches	Per dozen	$15.25		2 Knives, with Box,	30x 9 inches	Per dozen	$23.00
2 Knives, "	" 24x7 "	" "	16.00		3 " " "	30x 9 "	" "	25.00
3 " "	" 24x7 "	" "	18.50		4 " " "	30x 9 "	" "	27.00
4 " "	" 24x7 "	" "	20.50		2 " " "	36x12 "	Each	4.00
1 Knife,	" 26x8 "	" "	16.50		3 " " "	36x12 "	"	4.50
2 Knives,	" 26x8 "	" "	17.00		4 " " "	40x12 "	"	5.00
3 " "	" 26x8 "	" "	19.75		5 " " "	40x12 "	"	5.50
4 " "	" 26x8 "	" "	21.25		6 " " "	40x12 "	"	6.00

"ENTERPRISE" VEGETABLE SLICERS

This Machine is adapted to slicing all the different Vegetables, Fruits, etc., such as Cabbage for Sauerkraut and Coldslaw, Potatoes, Beets, Turnips, Carrots, Apples for Drying, Pineapples, Cucumbers, Eggplants, Pumpkins, Squashes, Onions, Citron, Rhubarb, Quinces, Melon Rind, Mangels for Cattle, etc. It is easily operated, and will be found a valuable kitchen implement for Hotels, Restaurants, Farmers, etc., etc.

Height, 16 inches; Diameter of Revolving Cylinder, 11 inches; Weight, 28 pounds.

No. 49 _____ Each $8.00

One in a Case.

NO. 49

"ENTERPRISE" SMOKED BEEF SHAVERS WITH SELF-SHARPENING DEVICE

SHARPENING DEVICE

NO. 23

The Knife is suspended pendulum-like, and each stroke cuts a slice cleanly and quickly, requiring but a few moments to shave down a pound of beef. The Automatic Feed can be regulated to cut from shavings as thin as tissue to slices one-eighth of an inch thick by adjusting small Bolt holding Connecting Rod.

No. 23 Japanned _____ Each $8.00

One in a Box.

NO. 125 AND 129, ROTARY

The Nos. 125 and 129 Rotary have about five and three times respectively the capacity of the No. 23. Will Cut slices of uniform thickness, from that of tissue paper to an eighth inch for the No. 125, and from 1-40th to ¼ inch for the No. 129, according as the Machine may be adjusted.

Height, 21 inches; Length, 30 inches; Width, 16 inches; Weight, 82 pounds.

No. **125** With 2 Blades _____ Each $22.50
" **129** " 1 Blade _____ " 22.50

One in a Crate.

From Biddle Hardware Co. Catalog, 1910

"ST. REGIS"
VEGETABLE SLICERS

SLAW CUTTERS
ADJUSTABLE KNIVES

FLUTED KNIFE

Reversible Handle Board, Cuts Plain Flutings, Lattice-Work and Shoe-String Potatoes.

"St. Regis," size, 4¾ x 13½ inches_____Per dozen $4.00

One dozen in a Box.

ONE KNIFE

Ajax, 1 Knife__Per dozen $3.00
Disston, 1 " _ " " 3.25

TWO KNIVES

Ajax, 2 Knives____Per dozen $4.50
Disston, 2 " ____ " " 6.00

THREE KNIVES

Disston, 3 Knives _____Per dozen $7.50

CROUT CUTTERS

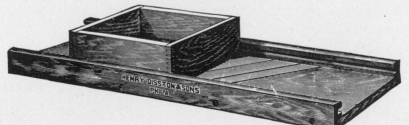

INDIANAPOLIS CROUT CUTTERS

No. **642** 2 Knives, 8 x 27 inches, Patent Sliding Box, Safety Lid_____Per dozen $16.70
" **643** 3 " 8 x 29 " " " " " " _____ " " 20.00
" **645** 3 " 9 x 33 " " " " " " _____ " " 30.00

Half dozen in a Crate.

DISSTON CROUT CUTTERS

1 Knife, with Box, 24 x 7 inches_____				Per dozen	$13.00
2 Knives, " " 24 x 7 " _____				" "	14.50
3 " " " 24 x 7 " _____				" "	16.50
4 " " " 24 x 7 " _____				" "	18.75
1 Knife, " " 26 x 8 " _____				" "	13.75
2 Knives, " " 26 x 8 " _____				" "	15.00
3 " " " 26 x 8 " _____				" "	18.00
4 " " " 6 x 8 " _____				" "	21.00
2 " " " 0 x 9 " _____				" "	20.00
3 " " " 30 x 9 " _____				" "	22.00
4 " " " 30 x 9 " _____				" "	24.25
2 " " " 36 x 12 " _____					3.75
3 " " " 36 x 12 " _____				" "	4.00
4 " " " 40 x 12 " _____				" "	5.00
5 " " " 40 x 12 " _____				" "	5.50
6 " " " 40 x 12 " _____				" "	6.00

From Biddle Hardware Co. Catalog, 1910

and was slid back and forth on a track against the curved grater. This was a widely advertised gadget, and one is still used today by the author to grate fresh nutmeg for holiday eggnog and for a topping on tapioca pudding.

Large and small graters were used for fruits and vegetables. Hand-pierced ones, alone or attached to a wooden back and handle, were artistically punched with dots and dashes. Stars were a favorite design. Victorian factory-made graters have a quaintness which bespeaks their age.

Cabbage cutters of wood with iron blades endured vigorous usage in the days of homemade sauerkraut and cole slaw. These wooden oddities have met their demise since the advent of wholesale making of sauerkraut (to be purchased in a can or plastic bag) and cole slaw (bought at a delicatessen). The cabbage slicers consisted of an oblong wooden frame with one or two metal cutting blades. Larger ones with a box or a compartment to hold the head of cabbage facilitated the making of sauerkraut. Sauerkraut required the shredding of dozens of heads to pack the barrel

From Biddle Hardware Co. Catalog, 1910

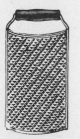

BREAD OR RADISH GRATERS
Wood Handle.

No	010	020
Sheet	¼	½
Inches	9x3	12x4
Per dozen	.62	.68

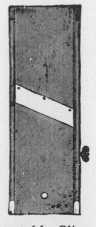

Vegetable Slicer.
1-blade 20 cts.   2-blade, 25 cts.
Can be regulated so as to cut thick or thin

From Van Heusen-Charles Co. Catalog, 1898

MINCING KNIVES.

25 to 50 cts.

or other container as tightly as possible since the cabbage shrinks in the brine as it processes. Hand-wrought blades and handmade wooden frames, especially of cherry, are the oldest and the most expensive. Patent-dated cutters are scarce.

Although some people do still use chopping knives and food grinders, it is rare to find someone who grates fresh nutmeg or makes his own sauerkraut.

Patented
Aug. 18,'91   Nov. 10,'96
Feb. 14,'99

The Edgar Nutmeg Grater

10 cts.   Saves all waste.

From Van Heusen-
Charles Co. Catalog, 1898

BOX GRATERS
2x5 inches.

No. 02 Plain _____ Per dozen .36

From Biddle Hardware
Co. Catalog, 1910

Clothes Irons

Irons have been made that were heated by placing hot coals, charcoal bricks, or metal slugs within them; by placing them on a hot surface; by the burning of gas or gasoline within them; and by passing an electrical current through their heating units. Old Chinese irons had an open metal bowl of pewter or brass and handles of wood. The reservoir was filled with hot coals, and the iron was moved in circles. Before the advent of the thermostatically controlled iron careful attention was needed to prevent scorching.

Some old American and European charcoal irons had a sliding drawer, a door that lifted with an arm, or a hinged opening in the back which was filled with hot coals or charcoal bricks. Some very attractive ones were made in brass with dark wooden handles. These were also called "box" irons. Slug irons were similar smoothing irons designed to hold a slug of metal that had been heated in the fireplace or on the stove. One nineteenth-century so-called "self-heating" charcoal iron was made of smooth cast iron with double flues. A metal shield protected the wooden handle and the user's hand from the heat. It was especially recommended for warm-weather ironing. However, since these irons weighed about fourteen pounds and took thirty minutes to heat, they would not be called efficient by modern standards.

The earliest flatirons or sadirons, "sad" meaning "heavy," were hand-wrought with their handles attached at only one spot. The typical nineteenth-century flatiron was made of heavy cast iron in several different weights, the numbers imprinted in the irons denoting their weight in pounds. The manufacturer's name was also sometimes cast into the iron. The handle was usually

Cont'd on page 81

SAD IRONS

COMMON											
Weight, pounds	4	5	6	7	8	9	Weight, pounds	5	6	7	8
Polished _____ Per pound	.06	.06	.06	.06	.06	.06	Nickel Plated _____ Per lb.	.08	.08	.08	.08

"ENTERPRISE" DOUBLE POINTED "STAR" IRONS

Stationary Handle, Japanned Handles and Caps. Made in three sizes—No. 1 with One End Rounded for Polishing, weight, 5 lbs.; No. 2 for General Use, weight, 5¾ lbs.; No. 3 for Heavy Work, weight, 6⅛ lbs.

No. 75 Polished, either No. 1, 2 or 3 __Per doz. $5.25

One or two dozen in a Case.

"ENTERPRISE" SQUARE BACK "STAR" IRONS

Stationary Handle, Japanned Handles and Caps. The Backs have Rounded Edges for Polishing. Made in three sizes—No.1 for Polishing, weight, 4¾ lbs.; No. 2 for General Use, weight, 5¾ lbs.; No. 3 for Heavy Work, weight, 6⅛ lbs.

No. 76 Polished, either No. 1, 2 or 3 __Per doz. $5.50

One or two dozen in a Case.

"ENTERPRISE" STAR POLISHING IRONS

Stationary Handle. Japanned Handles and Caps with All Round Edges.

No. 77 Polished, Weight 3 lbs _____Per doz. $5.25

One, two or three dozen in a Case.

"ENTERPRISE" CHINESE POLISHING IRONS

Cold Handle. Double Pointed, Japanned Caps and Stretchers.

No. 82 Nickel Plated, Weight 3   lbs __Per doz. $7.50
  " **80**   "   "   " 4½ " __ " " 9.25

One, two or three dozen in a Case.

From Biddle Hardware Co. Catalog, 1910

SAD IRONS

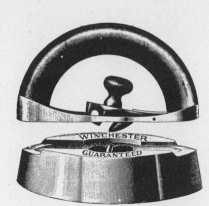

"WINCHESTER," NO. 450

Solid Iron, Full Nickel Plated on Top, Sides and Bottom; Nickel Plated Stretcher, Hardwood Handle, Nickel Plated Stand.

"Winchester" Three assorted sizes in a Set for Polishing, General Use and Heavy Work _____ Per set $1.90

Six Sets in a Case, with Stands.

NO. E55 AND E50
"ENTERPRISE," "MRS. POTTS'" IRONS

Cold Handle. Double Pointed. Three Irons, one Handle and Stand constitute a Set. No. 1, with One End Rounded for Polishing, weight, 4 lbs.; No. 2 for General Use, weight, $5\frac{3}{8}$ lbs.; No. 3 for Heavy Work, weight, $5\frac{1}{4}$ lbs. "Best" Handles with Forged Iron Stretchers.

No.	Per set.
E55 Polished, with Japanned Caps _____	$1.15
E55 " " Tinned " _____	1.15
E50 Nickel Plated, with Japanned Caps_____	1.20
E50 " " " Tinned " _____	1.20

One Set in a Package; Six Sets in a Case, with Stands.

NO. E65 AND E60
"ENTERPRISE," "MRS. POTTS'" IRONS

Cold Handle. Square Back with Rounded Edges for Polishing. Three Irons, one Handle and one Stand constitute a Set. No. 1, for Polishing, weight, $4\frac{1}{4}$ lbs.; No. 2 for General Use, weight, $4\frac{7}{8}$ lbs.; No. 3 for Heavy Work, weight, $5\frac{1}{4}$ lbs. "Best" Handles with Forged Iron Stretchers.

No.	Per set.
E65 Polished, with Japanned Caps _____	$1.35
E65 " " Tinned " _____	1.35
E60 Nickel Plated, with Japanned Caps_____	1.40
E60 " " " Tinned " _____	1.40

One Set in a Package; Six Sets in a Case, with Stands.

NO. E30, DOUBLE POINTED

NO. E40, SQUARE BACK

"ENTERPSISE" "MRS. POTTS'" NEW COLD HANDLE IRONS

These new Irons are Highly Polished and Nickel Plated, Tinned Caps or Top Plates. Each Set is equipped with the No. 200 Combination Handle described on page 751, thus despensing with a Stand.

No. E30 Nickel Plated, with No. 200 Combination Handles _____ Per set $1.75
" E40   "   "   "   "   " 200   "   " _____ " " 1.90

One Set in a Package; Six Sets in a Case.

From Biddle Hardware Co. Catalog, 1910

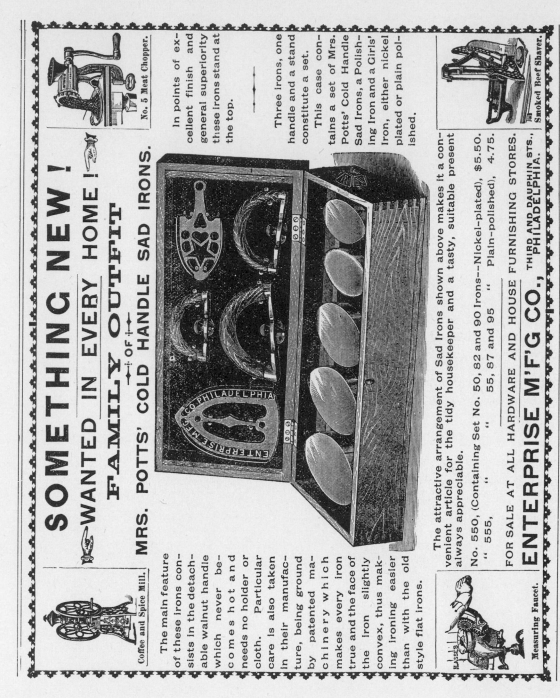

From Iron Age, Dec. 19, 1889

attached to the triangular-shaped base at two points. Sadirons were also made of triangles of heat-retaining soapstone attached to an iron frame or base and handle. These are considerably rarer than the cast-iron ones made in factories by the thousands.

Some old sadirons had a bell built into the handle. Legend states that the bell was placed there so the diligent housewife could hear if a servant stopped ironing. However, use reveals that the bell is barely audible, if at all, when the hand is over the handle. It was more likely just a whimsey.

Double-pointed irons had removable walnut or other hardwood handles. The famous "Mrs. Potts" sadirons were of this type. Some were sold in sets consisting of three pointed irons, one detachable handle, and one stand or trivet. Thus two irons could be heating as one was being used, and the handle could be removed from the cold iron and attached to a hot one. Some of these ferrosted steel irons were filled with asbestos to help keep the handles cool. A more elaborate ironing set contained three sadirons, a polishing iron, and a little girl's iron plus three different-sized clip-on handles and two trivets. All this came attractively packed in a wooden box. Such a set was made by The Enterprise Manufacturing Company.

Special irons were made of cast iron for specific purposes, such as fluting irons, sleeve irons, polish-

From U.S. Stamping Co. Catalog, Jan. 1883

GENEVA HAND FLUTERS.

	White Metal.	Brass.
Per Doz..................... ....12.00		15.00

POTTS'
IRON HANDLES AND STANDS

COMMON

Japanned	Per dozen	$1.25
Tinned	" "	1.50

"COLEBROOKDALE"

Wood Parts, Best Quality Gum. Strong Steel Spring, Long Heavy Screws, Fine Finish.

No. 10 Japanned	Per dozen	$1.50
" 20 Tinned	" "	1.75

"NEVER-BREAK"

All Steel, Japanned, Asbestos Washer.

Per dozen $1.75

"OBER"

Extra Quality Hardwood Handle, shaped so as to prevent cramping of the Hand. No Wooden Knob on Catch to break off.

No. 21 Nickel Plated .... Per dozen $1.75

"ENTERPRISE" NO. B 10

Handle is made of the Best Selected Wood, with a Forged Iron Stretcher attached with the longest and heaviest Screws possible.

No. B 10 With Tinned Iron Stretcher..Per doz. $2.50

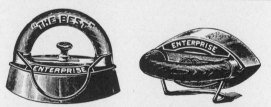

Position of Iron When in Use Position of Iron When Not in Use

"ENTERPRISE" COMBINATION HANDLES NO. 200

The addition of a Wire Side Rest serves the purpose of a Stand and also prevents the Iron when not in use from being scratched or defaced.

No. 200 With Tinned Iron Stretcher...Per doz. $3.00

SAD IRON STANDS

Per dozen .... .75

From Biddle Hardware Co. Catalog, 1910

SAD IRONS

"ENTERPRISE" FAMILY OUTFITS OF IRONS

No. 330 Containing No. 82, 90 and Set No. E50 Irons, as illustrated and described _____ $4.50

Six outfits in a Case.

ASBESTOS SAD IRONS

NO. 10, ASBESTOS

Consists of one Hood, one Oval 1 lb. Core. Face of Core, $4\frac{1}{4}$ x $1\frac{7}{8}$ inches. One Pressed Steel Stand.

No. **10** Tourist Iron_Per doz. $3.00

One in a Carton, twelve Cartons in a Case.

NO. 40, ASBESTOS

Consists of one Hood, one Oval 3 lb. Core. Face of Core, $4\frac{3}{4}$ x $2\frac{1}{2}$ inches. One Asbestos Covered Pressed Steel Stand.

No. **40** Sleeve Iron_Per doz. $6.00

One in a Carton, twelve Cartons in a Case.

NO. 50, ASBESTOS

Consists of one Hood, one Pointed 4 lb. Core. Face of Core, $6\frac{3}{4}$ x $2\frac{1}{2}$ inches

No. **50** Flounce Iron_Per doz. $7.20

One in a Carton, six Cartons in a Case.

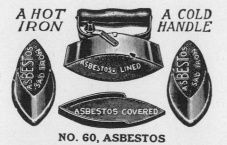

A HOT IRON   *A COLD HANDLE*

NO. 60, ASBESTOS

Consists of one Hood, two Oval 3 lb. Cores. Face of Cores, $4\frac{3}{4}$ x $2\frac{1}{2}$ inches. One Asbestos Covered Pressed Steel Stand.

No. **60** Shirt Waist Set_____Per dozen sets $9.00

One Set in a Wood Box, six Boxes in a Case.

A HOT IRON   *A COLD HANDLE*

NO. 70, ASBESTOS

Consists of one Hood, two Oval Cores, weight with Hood attached, 7 lbs. One Oval Core, weight with Hood attached, 6 lbs. Face of Cores, $6\frac{1}{2}$ x $3\frac{1}{4}$ inches. One Asbestos Covered Stand.

No. **70** Laundry Set _____Per dozen sets $21.00

One Set in a Wood Box, three or six Boxes in a Case.

From Biddle Hardware Co. Catalog, 1910

ing irons, and the tailor's goose. Fluting irons consisted of two corrugated parts, a stationary base piece and a movable hand piece. The base section was heated on the stove and then removed to an ironing board or table. The material to be ruffled was placed on the ridged base section and then pressed with the rolling or rocking hand piece. One such crimping iron was the Geneva Hand Fluter patented in 1866 in Geneva, Illinois. Other types of fluters worked by crank handles.

A sleeve iron was long and slender, pointed to suit its named purpose. Polishing irons were snub-nosed and particularly recommended for the pressing of shirt bosoms. Tailors used a large, long, heavy iron called a "tailor's goose," so-called because of its gooseneck handle. This special iron was for pressing woolens and weighs fifteen pounds or more.

Various gadgets were devised to help make the task of clothes ironing easier in the nineteenth century. Some sadiron stands were made with a sandpaper section for cleaning the plate of the iron and another section with a pad of beeswax for waxing it. Little packets of beeswax could be made or purchased for rubbing over the bottom of the iron to make it glide easier. Thick pads for protecting the hand from the hot metal handles of the sadirons were homemade or bought ready-made. Some flatiron handles were lined with a layer of soft, old leather to protect the hand.

Gasoline irons were smelly, dangerous, and extremely expensive, costing approximately eight times more than a good one-piece sadiron. They never became popular items because of these three disadavantages.

A convenience for the laundry of the city house was the gas iron. This was really a vented gas

TOY SAD IRONS

NO. 922

Polished and Nickel Plated, Detachable Hardwood Handle. Weight, 14 ounces each.

No. 922_____Per dozen $2.50

Half dozen in a Box, with Stands.

NO. 45

Polished and Nickel Plated, Detachable Hardwood Handle. Weight, 26 ounces each.

No. 45 _____Per dozen $4.50

One in a Box, with Stands.

NO. 90

"Enterprise," Cold Handle, Double Pointed, Detachable Handle, Japanned Caps and Stretchers. Weight, 1⅝ pounds.

No. 90 Nickel Plated_Per doz. $5.00

One dozen in a Case, with Stands.

TAILORS' GEESE

Weight, pounds	12	14	16	18
Size, inches	2¾x8⅜	2⅞x8⅞	3x9⅜	3⅛x9⅞
Open Handles Per pound	.11	.11	.11	.11
Closed " " "	.11	.11	.11	.11

Weight, pounds	20	22	24
Size, inches	3⅛x10	3¼x10⅜	3¼x11
Open Handles Per pound	.11	.11	.11
Closed " " "	.11	.11	.11

CHARCOAL IRONS

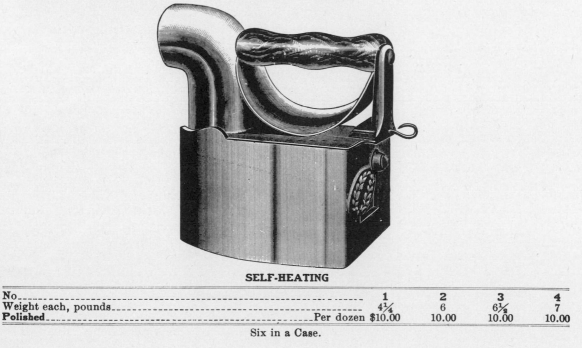

SELF-HEATING

No.	1	2	3	4
Weight each, pounds	4¼	6	6½	7
Polished Per dozen	$10.00	10.00	10.00	10.00

Six in a Case.

From Biddle Hardware Co. Catalog, 1910

From Good Housekeeping, Jan. 1921

stove with a tube attachment, and was so arranged that the flame could be regulated. It was considered cheaper to use a gas iron than to heat a sadiron on a gas range. These usually came equipped with six feet of rubber tubing to attach the iron to the gas outlet. A small, travel gas iron, patented in 1888, was constructed so that it could be heated over a regular gas jet, lifted off, and used.

The invention of the electric iron should go down as an important event in the history of homemaking. This new iron both lightened and cooled the task of clothes ironing.

The modern-day American is the biggest coffee-drinker in the world. Coffee has been used as a beverage in Arabia for at least 500 years. Coffeehouses were the favorite meeting places of many Europeans in the sixteenth and seventeenth centuries, and a coffeehouse was opened in Boston, Massachusetts, as early as 1670.

No doubt an especially designed coffee roaster was the best thing in which to roast coffee beans, but in early America not everyone had a coffee roaster. In *The Improved Housewife*, a cookbook written anonymously "by a married lady" in 1843, directions were given for drying and roasting coffee beans in an iron pot in the fireplace. Java and Mocha coffees were recommended as the best. By the method advised in this book the coffee beans were dried for three or four hours over a moderate fire. It was cautioned that the pot should be hung high to prevent burning. Then the coffee was roasted over a bed of hot coals as the cook constantly stirred the beans.

Tin roasters in both boxlike and cylindrical shapes were used in the preparation of coffee in the eighteenth century. These confined the

Cont'd on page 96

Coffee Roasters and Grinders

Tin coffee roaster with sliding door

COFFEE MILLS

BOX

NO. 950

Dimensions, 5½ x 5½ x 3¼ inches.

Castings, Brown Enameled Finish.

No. 950 Tin Hopper _____Per dozen $4.00

Six dozen in a Crate.

"MONITOR"

Bottom and Body are Drawn from a Single Piece of Sheet Steel. Seamless Steel Coffee Receptacle. Black Japanned Finish.

"Monitor," All Metal _____Per dozen $4.00

One dozen in a Case.

NO. 1088

Dimensions, 6 x 6 x 3¾ inches.

Castings, Black Japanned.

No. 1088 Raised Iron Hopper _____ Per dozen $5.50

Half dozen in a Box.

NO. 42

Dimensions, 6¾ x 6 x 5 inches.

Wood Bottom Drawer with Rounded Tin Sides. Castings, Coppered Finish, Cast Iron Swinging Cover, with Grasping Handle.

No. 42 Sunken Hopper _____Per dozen $8.25

Half dozen in a Box.

From Biddle Hardware Co. Catalog, 1910

COFFEE MILLS
BOX

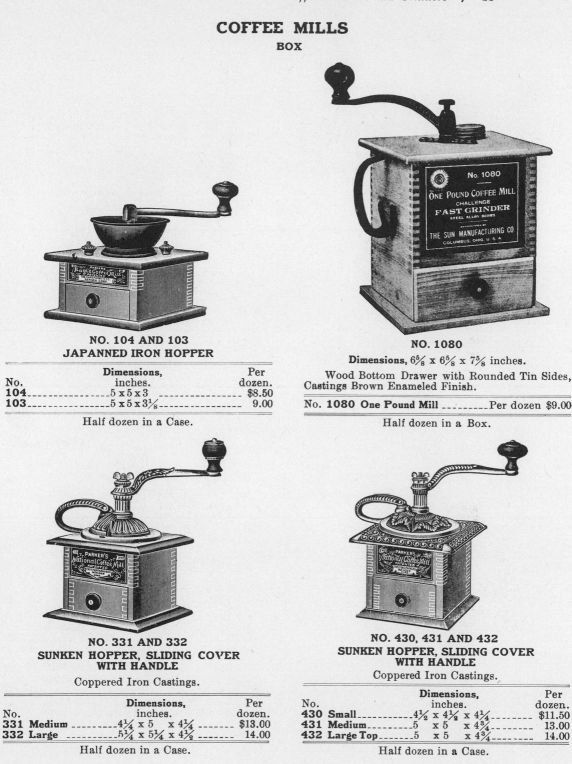

NO. 104 AND 103
JAPANNED IRON HOPPER

No.	Dimensions, inches.	Per dozen.
104	5 x 5 x 3	$8.50
103	5 x 5 x 3⅛	9.00

Half dozen in a Case.

NO. 1080

Dimensions, 6⅝ x 6⅝ x 7⅝ inches.

Wood Bottom Drawer with Rounded Tin Sides, Castings Brown Enameled Finish.

No. 1080 One Pound Mill	Per dozen $9.00

Half dozen in a Box.

NO. 331 AND 332
SUNKEN HOPPER, SLIDING COVER
WITH HANDLE

Coppered Iron Castings.

No.		Dimensions, inches.	Per dozen.
331	Medium	4¼ x 5 x 4¼	$13.00
332	Large	5¼ x 5¼ x 4½	14.00

Half dozen in a Case.

NO. 430, 431 AND 432
SUNKEN HOPPER, SLIDING COVER
WITH HANDLE

Coppered Iron Castings.

No.		Dimensions, inches.	Per dozen.
430	Small	4½ x 4½ x 4¼	$11.50
431	Medium	5 x 5 x 4¾	13.00
432	Large Top	5 x 5 x 4¾	14.00

Half dozen in a Case.

From Biddle Hardware Co. Catalog, 1910

COFFEE MILLS

BOX

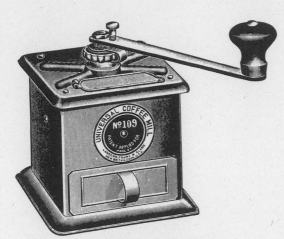

"UNIVERSAL," NO. 109

STEEL CASES, BLACK ENAMEL FINISH

Height, 6 inches.   Patent Adjusting Device.

No. **109** "Universal"_____Per dozen $12.00

Half dozen in a Case.

"UNIVERSAL," NO. 110

STEEL CASES, BLACK ENAMEL FINISH

Height, 8½ inches.   Patent Adjusting Device.

No. **110** "Universal"_____Per dozen $15.00

Half dozen in a Case.

NO. 25

JAPANNED IRON HOPPER, DOUBLE GRINDERS

Dimensions, 6⅛ x 6 x 4¼ inches.

No. **25** _____Per dozen $15.00

Half dozen in a Case.

NO. 35 AND 45

BRITANNIA HOPPER, DOUBLE GRINDERS

Dimensions, 6⅛ x 6 x 4¼ inches.

No.	Per dozen.
35 Varnished Boxes	$17.50
45 Black Walnut Boxes	18.00

Half dozen in a Case.

"CROWN," NO. 1

STEEL CASES, BLACK ENAMEL FINISH, BRASS SLIDING COVER

No.	Per dozen.
1 "Crown," 7 x 6 x 6 inches	$20.00

Half dozen in a Case.

From Biddle Hardware Co. Catalog, 1910

COFFEE MILLS
SIDE

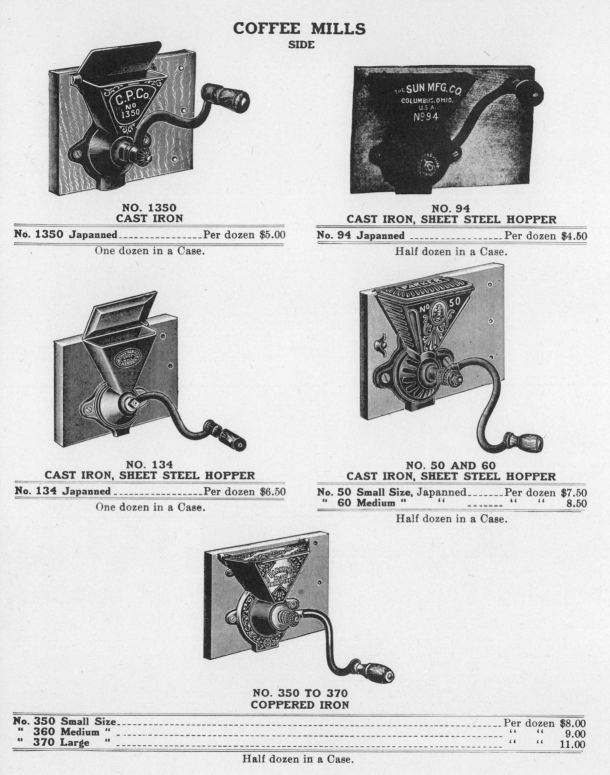

NO. 1350
CAST IRON

No. 1350 Japanned_____Per dozen $5.00

One dozen in a Case.

NO. 94
CAST IRON, SHEET STEEL HOPPER

No. 94 Japanned _____Per dozen $4.50

Half dozen in a Case.

NO. 134
CAST IRON, SHEET STEEL HOPPER

No. 134 Japanned_____Per dozen $6.50

One dozen in a Case.

NO. 50 AND 60
CAST IRON, SHEET STEEL HOPPER

No. 50 Small Size, Japanned_____Per dozen $7.50
  " **60** Medium " " _____ " " 8.50

Half dozen in a Case.

NO. 350 TO 370
COPPERED IRON

No. 350 Small Size		
No. 350 Small Size	Per dozen	$8.00
" **360** Medium "	" "	9.00
" **370** Large "	" "	11.00

Half dozen in a Case.

From Biddle Hardware Co. Catalog, 1910

"ENTERPRISE"
COFFEE MILLS

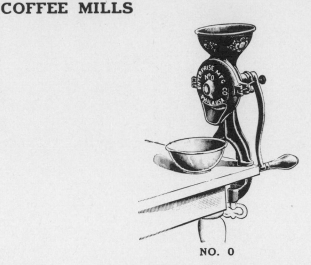

NO. 00

Capacity of Hopper, 4 ounces of Coffee. Grinds 6 ounces of Coffee per minute. Height, 9 inches. Weight, 6 pounds.

No. **00** _____Each $1.25

Twelve in a Case.

NO. 0

Capacity of Hopper, 4 ounces of Coffee. Grinds 6 ounces of Coffee per minute. Height 11½ inches. Weight, 6 pounds.

No. **0** _____Each $1.50

Twelve in a Case.

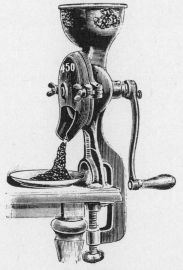

NO. 350

Capacity of Hopper, One Pound of Coffee. Grinds 12 ounces of Coffee per minute. Height 16⅝ inches. Weight, 17 pounds.

No. **350** _____Each $3.50

Three or Six in a Case.

NO. 450

Capacity of Hopper, One Pound of Coffee. Grinds 12 ounces of Coffee per minute. Height, 21 inches. Weight, 19½ pounds.

No. **450** _____Each $4.50

Three or Six in a Case.

From Biddle Hardware Co. Catalog, 1910

COFFEE MILLS
SIDE

"EVER READY," NO. 2

Sheet Steel Canister and Cup, Japanned Wood Back. Holds one pound of Coffee.

No. 2 "Ever Ready"_____Per dozen $7.00

One in a Carton; three dozen in a Crate.

"MAHOGANY," NO. 8

Sheet Steel Canister and Cup, Japanned, Heavy Oval Glass Front, Wood Back. Holds one pound of Coffee.

No. 8 "Mahogany"_____Per dozen $9.00

One in a Carton; one dozen in a Case.

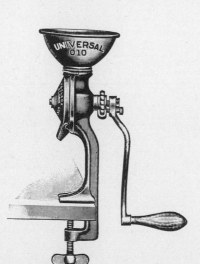

"UNIVERSAL," NO. 010

Sheet Steel Hopper, Black Enamel Finish. To Clamp on Table. Height, 11¼ inches.

No. 010 "Universal"_____Per dozen $11.00

Half dozen in a Case.

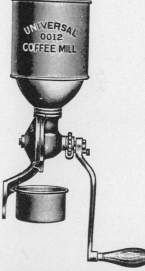

"UNIVERSAL," NO. 0012

Sheet Steel Canister and Cup, Black Enamel Finish. To Screw on Wall. Height, 13¼ inches.

No. 0012 "Universal" _____Per dozen $11.00

Half dozen in a Case.

From Biddle Hardware Co. Catalog, 1910

"ENTERPRISE"

COFFEE MILLS

NO. 1

NO. 2, 3 AND 5

NO. 2½, 4, 6, 8, 10 AND 210

NO. 7, 9 AND 209

No.	Capacity of Hoppers	Grinds per Minute	Hoppers	Height, inches	Diam. of Wheels, inches	Wgt., lbs.	Each
1	4 oz	6 oz	Iron	12½		10	2.25
2	4 "	6 "	"	12½	8¾	15	3.75
2½	7 "	6 "	Nickel Plated	15	8¾	14	5.00
3	½ lb	½ lb	Iron	15	10¾	22½	5.50
4	¾ "	½ "	Nickel Plated	20½	10¾	22	8.00
5	¾ "	¾ "	Iron	17	12½	36	8.00
6	1¾ "	¾ "	Nickel Plated	24	12½	35	12.00
7	1¾ "		Iron	21½	17	62	11.00
8	2¼ "		Nickel Plated	27	17	59	16.00
9	3 "		Iron	24	19½	107	16.00
209	5 "		"	33	25	156	24.00
10	4½ "		Nickel Plated	28	19½	102	21.00
210	4½ "		" "	37	25	147	30.00

NUMBER OF TURNS REQUIRED TO GRIND ONE POUND OF COFFEE, NO. 7 TO 210

For No	7	8	9	209	10	210
Turns	75	75	75	50	75	50

PACKED AS FOLLOWS

No	1	2	2½	3	4	5	6
In Case	6	6	6	3	1	3	1

No	7	8	209	10	210
In Crate	1	1 Crate 1 Box	1	1 Crate 1 Box	1 Crate 1 Box

From Biddle Hardware Co. Catalog, 1910

"ENTERPRISE" COFFEE MILLS

NO. 12 AND 212

No.	Capacity of Hoppers	Hoppers	Height	Diameter of Wheels	Weight	Each.
12	5 lbs	Iron	32 in	25 in	141 lbs	$24.00
212	6½ "	"	43 "	31 "	211 "	35.00

Fifty turns will Grind one Pound of Coffee.
No. 12, One in a Crate; No 212, in Two Crates and One Box.

"BLACK HAWK" GRIST MILLS

For Farm and Family use.

Malleable Iron Crank, Chilled Bearings, Grinding Burrs of the Hardest and Strongest Metal.

"Black Hawk," Weight, 17 lbs _____Each $4.00

"ENTERPRISE" BONE, SHELL AND CORN MILLS

NO. 650

NO. 750 With Fly Wheel
" 550 " Crank

CAPACITY, 1¼ BUSHELS OF CORN PER HOUR

These Mills are especially adapted for grinding Bones (when **dry** only), Oyster and other Shells, Corn, Roots, Bark, Grain, Salt, etc.

No.		Height	Length	Width	Dimensions of Throat	Diameter of Wheel	Weight	Each.
550	With Crank	17¼ in	12 in	8½ in	3x2 in	No Wheel	42 lbs	$7.00
650	With Fly Wheel	11 "	12 "	9 "	3x2 "	19 in.	47½ "	7.50
750	" " "	17¼ "	12 "	8½ "	3x2 "	19 "	60 "	8.50

One in a Crate.

From Biddle Hardware Co. Catalog, 1910

aromatic flavor of the coffee and produced a much better tasting beverage than that from roasting by the iron-pot method. The cylindrical roaster was formed of tin near one end of a long iron rod. The short projecting iron point was rested on the hearth close to the fire, and the roaster was rotated by its long handle. Most cylindrical roasters had sliding covers which moved in grooved slots. Roasting the coffee beans took considerable skill, for too little or too much roasting ruined the flavor. Since airtight containers were a rarity, the coffee had to be used soon after its roasting or it lost its flavor.

With the advent of the coal stove special coffee-bean roasters were devised, so constructed that they fitted into one of the round openings on the stove top. A crank handle on the top of the roaster was turned to keep the beans moving and thus prevent scorching.

After roasting, the beans were ground in a coffee grinder or mill—the earliest mills being handmade wrought-iron ones screwed to the wall. Later, cast-iron ones were made in this same design. The "Ever-Ready" coffee mill manufactured by the Bronson Walton Company of Cleveland, Ohio, had a sheet-steel canister which held one pound of coffee. Grinders with sheet-steel hoppers were designed to be clamped on the table. Large table-model grinders were manufactured for store use. The familiar wooden-box-type grinder was made in dozens of models by many manufacturers, some with britannia hoppers or brass covers. A few models with patented adjusting devices had black enameled steel cases.

Early American cooks sometimes put a piece of isinglass or fish skin into the coffee when it was put to boil. The skin of mild codfish was suggested. Later-day cooks used the white of an egg or an eggshell for the same clarifying effect.

Before the invention of the crank eggbeater, eggs were beaten with a two- or three-tined fork, a wire whisk, a narrow-slotted wooden paddle, or a miniature splintered birch broom.

There were many models of patent-dated rotary-crank eggbeaters. A rather primitive tin and iron one, called the "Dover Eggbeater," was patented in 1878. The Taplin and the similar Cyclone and Holt models were all patented between 1899 and 1908. The Cyclone had the unique feature of perforated blades.

All of these patented eggbeaters were well advertised. Holt's beater was touted as "guaranteed to whip a pint of cream fine in two or three minutes and to beat eggs in twenty seconds. We guarantee it to beat eggs or whip cream in one third the time of the best Dover beater. It is larger and stronger than the best Dover beater and has improved flaring dashers." It came in a 10½-inch

Eggbeaters and Cream Whippers

Left to right: Betty Taplin beater, 5½ in. long; beater marked "Beats anything in a cup or bowl," 7 in. long; Baby Bingo No. 68 beater, 5½ in. long

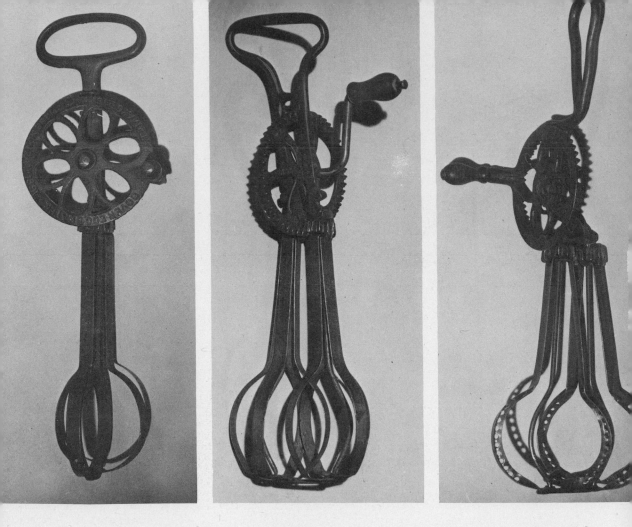

Left to right: The Dover beater, patented 1878; the Taplin beater, patented 1908; the Cyclone beater, patented 1901

From Good Housekeeping, a 1924 issue

family size and a 12½-inch hotel size. These early eggbeaters all had heavy iron cranks and handles and tinned blades. The various attractive designs on the crankwheels in the shapes of hearts, flowers, and other motifs were interesting in themselves.

A lightweight all-tin beater was patented in 1926 and was much the same as its modern counterpart. One of the same patent came fitted with a glass bowl and tin cover to prevent splattering on an energetic high-speed operator.

Push-handle whippers were patented in 1900, their wooden handles so designed as to be gripped in the fist and pushed up and down. The use of these models was apt to tip over the bowl. Modern

ones almost identical to this original are still made
and used.

A galvanized wire eggbeater was operated by
a side-mounted thumb lever. The spindle blades
twirled one way then the other. This is a rather
rare model, even though not so old, dating from
the turn of the century.

A post-Civil War combination eggbeater-cream
whipper consisted of two parts. It was made of
heavy tinplate with an iron handle and was one
of several slightly different designs in this type.
One was marked "patented 1868"; another was
stamped "Lightning Cream Whip and Egg
Beater." Whip churns or "syllabub churns," as
these were called, were recommended by Fannie

*From Biddle Hardware
Co. Catalog, 1910*

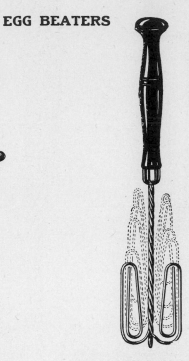

Left to right: Merry
Whirl beater, patented
Nov. 28, 1916; the A & J
beater with glass bowl,
patented 1923; push-
handle whipper patented
in England 1935;
American-made push-
handle whipper

"DOVER"

Family Size.

No. 75 ------Per dozen $1.40

One dozen in a Box.

"A & J"

Egg Beater, Cream Whip and
Mayonnaise Mixer. Operated
with One Hand by a Short Up
and Down Stroke. Polished
Hardwood Handle, Enameled
Finish. Tinned Wire Wings.
Steel Ferrule, Nickel Plated.

No. 1 Family Size. Per doz. $4.00

One dozen in a Box.

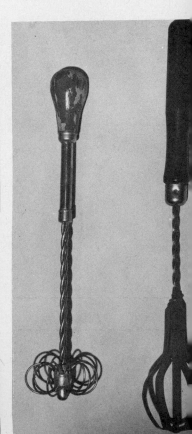

Merritt Farmer in her 1896 edition of *The Boston Cooking-School Cook Book* for whipping thin cream or heavy cream diluted with milk.

The procedure for using a whip churn was to place the cylinder on the bottom of the bowl containing eggs or cream. Holding the cylinder still with one hand, the user whipped the rod section up and down with the other hand, a tiresome task but eventually effective. Of a similar appearance was a closed tin container with a loose rod and wheels inside which was to be shaken much as a cocktail shaker, the loose mechanism inside hastening the whipping process. This was more fittingly called a cream shaker.

From Van Heusen-Charles Co. Catalog, 1898

Syllabub Churn.
For Whipping Cream.
15 cts. to 40 cts.

The Improved Mayonnaise Mixer and Egg Beater Combined.

$1.25.

PATENT.

EGG AND CREAM BEATER.

$1.25

From Van Heusen-Charles Co. Catalog, 1898

Whip churn. *Left and right:* Unassembled churn. *Center:* Assembled churn stamped "Lightning Cream Whip and Egg Beater," patented 1868, manufactured in Albany, New York

A tin boxlike beater for eggs or cream was operated by a crank-handle on its side. Turning the handle rapidly twirled the wire paddle wheel inside. This contrivance could also be used to make a small batch of homemade butter.

The ingenuity and progress of the American people is evidenced even in their humble beaters and whippers.

SYLLABUB CHURNS.

Per Doz...3.50

From U.S. Stamping Co. Catalog, Jan. 1883

Eggs were definitely on the menu in America in the eighteenth century. However, they were not as popular at breakfast as at dinner and supper, our usual bacon and eggs being a more modern breakfast. Deviled eggs and a curious recipe for "an egg as big as twenty" were recipes found in eighteenth-century cookbooks. Of course, many eggs, as well as much Jamaican rum, rye, or bourbon whiskey, were used in the familiar eggnog of yore. English cookbooks were much used in America in both the eighteenth and nineteenth centuries; the latter employed eggs in their recipes for Christmas pudding and savory omelets of all kinds. Boiled and poached eggs were an English favorite, utilizing turkey eggs as well as hen and duck eggs. Egg balls made of the mashed yolks of hard boiled eggs mixed with a raw egg yolk, flour, parsley, salt, and pepper and then rolled into small balls and boiled for two minutes were listed in *The Improved Housewife or Book of Receipts* printed in 1846 in Hartford, Connecticut.

Egg separators are interesting little items which could prove difficult for the uninformed to identify. They were actually contrivances for separating the yolk of the egg from the white portion as for use in certain recipes. Most of these were of nine-

Egg Separators, Poachers, and Boilers

Two tin egg separators with advertising. *Center*: Pewter egg scissors, probably German

Left: Two aluminum egg separators. *Right*: Mid-twentieth-century plastic separator.
Center: Note double ears for resting on bowl

From F. A. Walker & Co. Catalog, 1886

No. 658.
Table Egg Boiler, with Alcohol Lamp.
4, 6, 8 eggs.
Brass, Copper, Nickel.

teenth-century and early twentieth-century manufacture, and were made of tin or aluminum. The pressed-tin ones served as inexpensive and useful advertising media when embossed with slogans and product trade names. Favorite advertisers were fuel, furnace, and range companies. Rumford Baking Powder gave one as a premium. Modern-day plastic egg separators still act as such business sponsors, and a spritely one advises "good eggs to do business with." The old tin ones usually were impressed, in tiny letters, "egg separator" just to be certain their purpose was made known. Most of these tin ones seem to have been made in Chicago.

Another late nineteenth-century egg accessory was the table egg boiler. These were devices for hard- or soft-boiling eggs right at the dining table. They boiled four, six, eight, or ten eggs at a time and were made of brass, copper, or nickel. Some cooked the eggs by simply filling the vessel with boiling water, while others were heated by an attached alcohol lamp. Inner racks held the eggs in place. Table egg boilers were usually quite ornate with scrolls and fancy feet. One especially attractive one was shaped, appropriately, in the form of a very large egg.

A simple gadget for boiling eggs on the stove in a cookpot was a folding wire holder which encompassed six eggs in individual rings. It was made entirely of wire and allowed the half dozen eggs to be immersed and removed from the boiling water at one time. One such boiler bears the unlikely advertisement of a lumber company! A large top-of-the-stove egg cooker was an oval-shaped vessel made of copper or of sheet iron with a platform attached to the lid which kept the eggs raised in the boiling water. Eggs in the nineteenth century seemed to have harder shells than those of today and were especially well suited to boiling in the shell.

For poaching eggs neatly, there was a round perforated tin appliance with a handle and six collar rings to encircle the poached eggs and keep them compactly in shape. A spring-operated thumb lever lifted up the rings and allowed the

EGG BOILERS.
For Use on Dining Tables.
8-egg, $1.50.   10-egg, $1.75.

*From Van Heusen-
Charles Co. Catalog, 1898*

Wire egg boiler; lumber
company advertising
on handle

*From U.S. Stamping Co.
Catalog, Jan. 1883*

Aluminum "Acme" egg-
grading scale,
patented 1924

eggs to slide smoothly and intact from the apparatus to the serving plate. One egg poacher had shell-shaped impressions for the eggs.

Egg drainers made of tin, silver, horn, porcelain, or wood were large skimmer-type spoons with holes used for lifting poached eggs from the cooking pan. The holes allowed the water to drain away. Some of the old tin catalogs from the late 1800s called these tin egg drainers "egg poachers."

Elegant egg stands in silver-plated ware served the cooked soft- or hard-boiled eggs on the dining table. Most of these were of English manufacture, and some had slots for holding the individual spoons as well as cups for the eggs.

Egg scales were used for grading eggs according to their weight. Although not a cooking implement, egg scales were employed by many old-time farm wives for grading their eggs for sale, and hence many were found in the late nineteenth- and early twentieth-century kitchens. The Acme Egg Grading Scale, patented June 24, 1924, was made of aluminum on a sheet-iron base. Most egg scales were japanned tin with the grading scales imprinted on the sides.

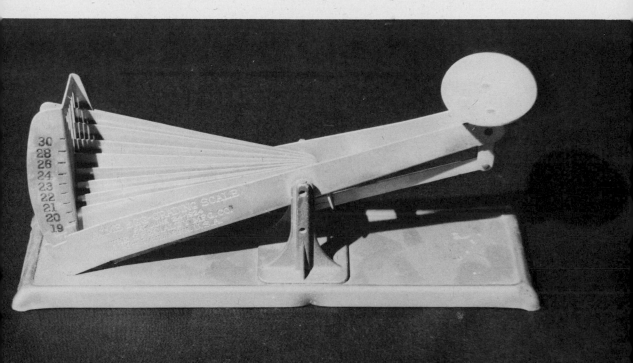

Graniteware was a nineteenth-century innovation in cookware. This new cooking material was iron with an enameled coating and was called variously "enamelware," "granite ironware," "glazed-ware," "granite steelware," and "agateware." This last name was especially suitable as the mottling on this cookware resembled the mineral agate. It was advertised as a wholesome, serviceable, and durable cookingware, unaffected by acid foods and easy to clean. Original ads for this ware highlighted its safety for use in cooking, for drinking vessels, and for other purposes.

This newly invented ware was featured at the Philadelphia Centennial Exposition of 1876. It was touted to combine "the advantages of glass with the strength of metal." It was proclaimed to be "light, elegant, clean, and everlasting." As compared to the heavy, old, cast-iron pots and kettles, it certainly was lightweight. The smooth,

Graniteware

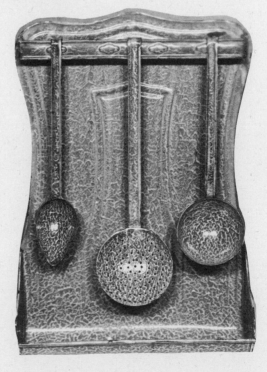

Graniteware flask and kitchen-tool set in hanging rack. *Courtesy of The Rusty Naill, Hanover, Pa.*

Rare gray graniteware cruet set. *Courtesy of The Rusty Naill, Hanover, Pa.*

hard surface was definitely easier to clean than iron, copper, tin, or brass. However, it was surely not everlasting. Nowadays it is quite rare to find an old piece without a chip or two!

The most intriguing shapes in graniteware kitchen goods were the quaint coffeepots and teapots, bearing such refined names as the "Imperial" coffeepot and the "Belle" teapot. Some quite elaborate models had white metal spouts, handles, and lids with decorative finials. There were graniteware saucepans, pots, rice or milk boilers, farina boilers, and cruller and potato friers with a perforated inner pot. Attractively shaped, oval butter kettles had fanciful lid knobs of white metal. Preserving kettles of graniteware were popular in the late 1800s because of the ware's resistance to acid. There were griddles, broilers, shallow stew pans, colanders, scoops, dippers, basting spoons, skimmers, pie plates, fry pans, flasks, water buckets, wine coolers, and muffin pans.

Daintier graniteware items included the cake molds in octagon, turban, and turk's-head shapes and a variety of tube cake pans. Cake molds having twelve sides were called dodecahedral molds. For the table there were cups, mugs, saucers, tumblers, children's mugs, trays, soup bowls, meat dishes, and even dinner plates and alphabet-embossed plates for the children.

Graniteware toilet articles included slop jars, chamber pails and pots, foot tubs, water carriers, water pitchers and bowls, and soap dishes, some hanging and some with covers. Candlestick holders were produced in a variety of shapes and sizes. Two rare items of special interest were cruet-set holders with glass condiment containers and a matching set of a wall rack with an assortment of hanging utensils.

Cont'd on page 119

From *McClure's Magazine, Aug. 1904*

"EL-AN-GE" ENAMELED WARE

MOTTLED GRAY ENAMEL

IMPROVED SEAMLESS FAMILY COLANDERS
With Fast Feet.

No. **1205** 10 x 4 inches _____Per dozen $6.75

WASH BASINS, WITH RINGS

No	26	28	30	32
Inches	$10\frac{3}{8}$x$2\frac{3}{4}$	$11\frac{3}{8}$x$2\frac{7}{8}$	$12\frac{1}{4}$x$3\frac{1}{8}$	13x$3\frac{3}{8}$
Per dozen	$3.00	3.35	3.85	4.50

SHALLOW PIE PLATES

No	9	10	11
Inches	9x$\frac{7}{8}$	10x1	11x1
Per dozen	$2.10	2.40	3.00

DEEP PIE PLATES

Inches	9
Per dozen	$2.75

SEAMLESS WATER PAILS
Flat Bottom.

No	108	110	112
Quarts	8	10	12
Inches	$9\frac{1}{2}$x$6\frac{3}{4}$	$10\frac{1}{2}$x$7\frac{3}{4}$	$11\frac{1}{2}$x$8\frac{3}{4}$
Per dozen	$10.00	11.00	13.00

DRINKING CUPS

No	9	10	11
Inches	4x$2\frac{1}{2}$	$4\frac{1}{4}$x$2\frac{3}{4}$	$4\frac{1}{2}$x3
Per dozen	$2.00	2.25	2.50

SEAMLESS STRAIGHT CUPS

No	0
Pint	$\frac{1}{2}$
Inches	$3\frac{1}{4}$x2
Per dozen	$2.25

SOUP LADLES

No. **38,** With Threaded Handle, $3\frac{1}{2}$x$1\frac{5}{8}$ inches,
Per dozen $2.50

WALL SOAP DISHES, WITH GRATES

No. **60** $6\frac{1}{2}$x4x$1\frac{1}{2}$ inches _____Per dozen $3.00

THREADED BASTING SPOONS

Length, inches	12	14
Per dozen	$1.75	2.00

From Biddle Hardware Co. Catalog, 1910

"ONYX" ENAMELED WARE
FIRST GRADE
RICH BROWN ENAMEL HEAVILY MOTTLED WITH WHITE

TEA POTS

Retinned Covers, Enameled Iron Handles, Wood Knobs.

No.	11	12	13	14
Quarts	1½	2	3	4
Per dozen	$8.50	9.50	10.50	11.50

COFFEE POTS

Retinned Covers, Enameled Iron Handles, Wood Knobs.

No.	11½	12½	13½	14½
Quarts	1½	2	3	4
Per dozen	$8.00	9.00	10.00	11.00

COFFEE BOILERS

Retinned Covers, Wood Knobs, Wood Handle on Bail.

No.	70	80
Quarts	6	8
Per dozen	$15.00	18.00

TEA KETTLES

Enameled Covers, Wood Knobs, Lock Bail, Wood Handle.

No.	7	8
Quarts	5	7
Per dozen	$15.00	17.50

UNIVERSAL CEREAL COOKERS

Retinned Covers, Wood Knobs, Wood Handle on Bail.

No.	020	030	040
Quarts (Inside Boiler)	2	3	4
Per dozen	$10.25	13.50	16.50

SEAMLESS FLARING WATER PAILS
Wood Handle on Bail.

No.	210	212
Quarts	11	12½
Inches	11⅛ x 8¾	11⅞ x 9⅛
Per dozen	$14.00	16.00

From Biddle Hardware Co. Catalog, 1910

From *American Monthly,
Review of Reviews,
Oct. 1900*

From *Munsey's
Magazine, Mar. 1898*

AGATE IRON WARE.

BERLIN KETTLES.
45 cts. to $1.00.

PRESERVING KETTLES.
30 cts. to $1.60.

The superiority of Agate Iron Ware over all other makes of culinary utensils consists largely in the fact that the enamel is so hard that the fusing point is not reached until the iron of which the articles are formed is about ready to melt, thereby combined with the pure vitreous composition and forming a clinch or perfect union, which no subsequent heating can destroy, and which for tenacity and power to resist the action of acids has no equal.

The purity of the materials used in its composition, the excellency of the workmanship, together with the finish and multiplicity of designs and shapes, are such that it enjoys a world-wide reputation.

The ware is strong and durable, yet light and convenient to handle, and the surface being hard and smooth, is as easily cleaned as china. Altogether it is the purest, cleanest, most durable and best ware for family use ever made. It will not rust, break or solve like ordinary enamels, and is absolutely pure and safe to use, as certified to by the most eminent chemists here and abroad.

LIPPED SAUCEPAN.
20 cts. to 55 cts.

TEAPOTS.
45 cts. to 85 cts.

TEAKETTLES.
95 cts. to $1.85.

WINE COOLER.
$1.00.

From Van Heusen-Charles Co. Catalog, 1898

"TURQUOISE" ENAMELED WARE
EXTRA QUALITY
BLUE AND WHITE MOTTLED FINISH ON OUTSIDE, PURE WHITE INSIDE

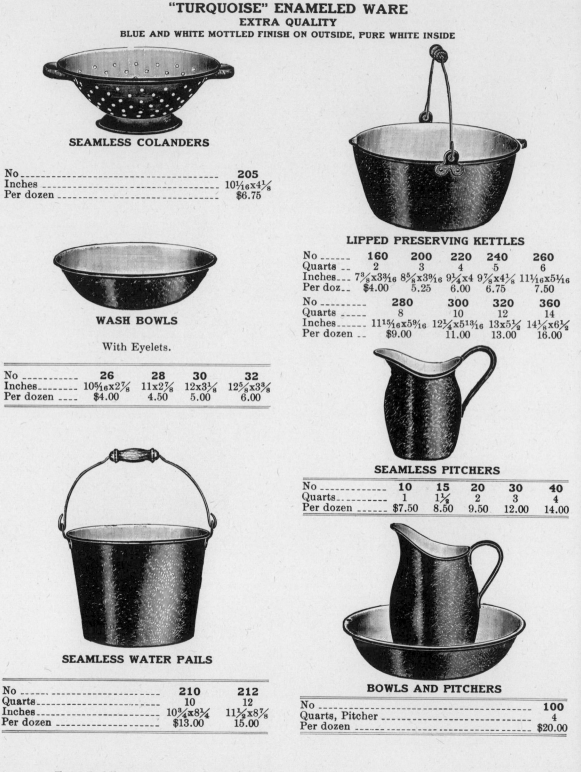

SEAMLESS COLANDERS

No	205
Inches	$10\frac{1}{16}$x$4\frac{1}{8}$
Per dozen	$6.75

WASH BOWLS

With Eyelets.

No	26	28	30	32
Inches	$10\frac{9}{16}$x$2\frac{7}{8}$	11x$2\frac{7}{8}$	12x$3\frac{1}{8}$	$12\frac{5}{8}$x$3\frac{3}{8}$
Per dozen	$4.00	4.50	5.00	6.00

LIPPED PRESERVING KETTLES

No	160	200	220	240	260
Quarts	2	3	4	5	6
Inches	$7\frac{3}{8}$x$3\frac{3}{16}$	$8\frac{5}{8}$x$3\frac{9}{16}$	$9\frac{1}{4}$x4	$9\frac{7}{8}$x$4\frac{1}{8}$	$11\frac{1}{16}$x$5\frac{1}{16}$
Per doz.	$4.00	5.25	6.00	6.75	7.50

No	280	300	320	360
Quarts	8	10	12	14
Inches	$11\frac{15}{16}$x$5\frac{9}{16}$	$12\frac{1}{4}$x$5\frac{13}{16}$	13x$5\frac{1}{2}$	$14\frac{1}{8}$x$6\frac{1}{2}$
Per dozen	$9.00	11.00	13.00	16.00

SEAMLESS PITCHERS

No	10	15	20	30	40
Quarts	1	$1\frac{1}{2}$	2	3	4
Per dozen	$7.50	8.50	9.50	12.00	14.00

SEAMLESS WATER PAILS

No	210	212
Quarts	10	12
Inches	$10\frac{3}{4}$x$8\frac{1}{4}$	$11\frac{1}{2}$x$8\frac{7}{8}$
Per dozen	$13.00	15.00

BOWLS AND PITCHERS

No	100
Quarts, Pitcher	4
Per dozen	$20.00

From Biddle Hardware Co. Catalog, 1910

"ONYX" ENAMELED WARE
FIRST GRADE
RICH BROWN ENAMEL, HEAVILY MOTTLED WITH WHITE

IMPROVED DEEP DISH PANS
Hollow Steel Handles, Fit the Hand.

Quarts	10	14	17	21
Inches	$13\frac{5}{8}$x$4\frac{1}{4}$	$15\frac{5}{8}$x$5\frac{1}{4}$	$17\frac{1}{8}$x$5\frac{1}{4}$	$18\frac{1}{8}$x6
Per dozen	$11.00	13.00	15.00	18.00

WASH BASINS

No	26	28	30	32
Quarts	$2\frac{1}{4}$	$2\frac{3}{4}$	$3\frac{1}{2}$	$4\frac{1}{4}$
Inches	$10\frac{3}{8}$x$2\frac{3}{4}$	$11\frac{1}{4}$x$2\frac{3}{4}$	$11\frac{7}{8}$x$3\frac{1}{8}$	$12\frac{1}{2}$x$3\frac{3}{8}$
Per dozen	$4.00	4.50	5.00	6.00

EXTRA DEEP PUDDING PANS
Round Edge.

No	16	17	18	19	20	21	22
Quarts	1	$1\frac{1}{2}$	2	3	4	5	6
Inches	$7\frac{3}{8}$x$2\frac{1}{4}$	$8\frac{1}{8}$x$2\frac{7}{16}$	$8\frac{1}{2}$x$2\frac{3}{4}$	$9\frac{1}{4}$x3	$9\frac{3}{4}$x$3\frac{1}{8}$	$10\frac{3}{4}$x$3\frac{3}{8}$	$11\frac{1}{2}$x$3\frac{5}{8}$
Per dozen	$3.00	3.25	3.75	4.00	4.50	5.00	6.00

JELLY CAKE PANS
Extra Deep.

Inches	9	10
Per dozen	$3.00	3.50

PIE PLATES
Deep.

Inches	9	10
Per dozen	$2.75	3.25

MILK KETTLES

Retinned Covers with Handle.
Wood Handles on Bails.

Quarts	1	2
Per dozen	$6.00	7.50

DRINKING CUPS
Staple Sizes.

			Seamed.
No	9	10	7
Pints	$\frac{1}{2}$	$\frac{3}{4}$	$\frac{3}{4}$
Inches	$4\frac{1}{8}$x$2\frac{1}{4}$	$4\frac{3}{8}$x$2\frac{1}{2}$	$4\frac{1}{8}$x$2\frac{1}{2}$
Per doz.	$2.00	2.25	2.00

SOUP LADLES
Extra Deep Bowls.

No	38
Inches	$3\frac{1}{2}$x$1\frac{5}{8}$
Per dozen	$2.50

CHAMBERS
Wide Flange. Enameled Covers.
Wood Knobs.

	Chambers only.	Covers only.
No	2	2
Quarts	$4\frac{1}{2}$	
Inches	$9\frac{3}{8}$x$5\frac{1}{8}$	
Per dozen	$9.00	4.00

WALL SOAP DISHES

Corrugated Bottoms.

No	60
Inches	$6\frac{1}{2}$x$4\frac{1}{2}$x$1\frac{1}{4}$
Per dozen	$2.50

BASTING SPOONS
Heavy Threaded Handles.

Inches	12	14
Per dozen	$1.75	2.00

WINDSOR DIPPERS
Round Edge.

No	412
Quart	1
Inches	$5\frac{1}{4}$x$2\frac{3}{4}$
Per dozen	$4.50

From Biddle Hardware Co. Catalog, 1910

"The Secret of Successful Preserving~"

says the practical housewife,

—"is choice fruit, accurate measuring *and a good kettle*—and I don't know but what the last is the most important, because so much depends upon the *cooking*."

A scientifically constructed, carefully proportioned, heat-retaining OLD ENGLISH Kettle will be a big help to you in your canning this summer. It will be a real factor in the success of the jams, jellies and preserves in which you take so much pride, as every woman does!

Old English enameled ware is *unusually* high grade; and enameled ware is conceded by health authorities and culinary experts to be unexcelled for all forms of cooking—particularly boiling and stewing—because its glistening, porcelain-like surface is protection for liquids or semi-liquids such as ketchup or jelly, or other foods containing beneficial acids or alkalis.

OLD ENGLISH Kettles are made from extra heavy gauge steel—beautifully and uniformly enameled in a handsome light gray mottle, clean and sanitary, and finished with a high gloss.

Will last for many years—and serve in many ways. In addition to canning and preserving, an OLD ENGLISH Kettle can be used for making soup, boiled dinners, lemonade and pop corn balls, and in the fall no better vessel can be found in which to make apple or peach butter, render lard, etc.

Made in 7 sizes, from 7 quart to 24 quart (full capacity) and sold by the better stores whose buyers are the shrewdest judges of value. Write for our free Preserving Schedule for the housewife.

THE
IDENTIFYING
LABEL

THE REPUBLIC STAMPING & ENAMELING CO., CANTON, OHIO

TRADE MARK

From Good Housekeeping, July 1923

"TURQUOISE" ENAMELED WARE

EXTRA QUALITY

BLUE AND WHITE MOTTLED FINISH ON OUTSIDE, PURE WHITE INSIDE

SEAMLESS COVERED BUCKETS
Enameled Covers.

No	10	20	30	40
Quarts	1	2	3	4
Inches	5¹⁄₁₆x3⁷⁄₁₆	6⁵⁄₁₆x4⁹⁄₁₆	6¹³⁄₁₆x5⅛	7¾x5½
Per dozen	$6.00	7.00	8.50	10.50

SEAMLESS MILK KETTLES
Tin Covers.

No	71	72
Quarts	1	2
Per dozen	$7.50	10.00

DEEP DRINKING CUPS

No	8	9	10
Pints	½	¾	1
Inches	3½x2¹⁄₁₆	3⅞x2⁵⁄₁₆	4¹⁄₁₆x2⁹⁄₁₆
Per doz	$1.75	2.00	2.25

SEAMLESS STRAIGHT CUPS

No	0	6
Pints	½	1
Inches	3½x2⅝	3⅞x2⁹⁄₁₆
Per dozen	$2.25	3.00

DEEP STRAIGHT CUPS

No	100
Inches	4¹³⁄₁₆x4⁹⁄₁₆
Pints	2
Per dozen	$5.00

FLARING DIPPERS

Flat Handles.

No	011	012
Inches	4⁹⁄₁₆x2½	4⅞x2¹⁵⁄₁₆
Per dozen	$2.75	3.00

WINDSOR DIPPERS
Improved Round Enameled Handles.

No	110
Quarts	1
Inches	5x2¾
Per dozen	$4.00

COCOA DIPPERS

No	55
Inches	3⅞x3⅛
Pints	1
Per dozen	$5.00

From Biddle Hardware Co. Catalog, 1910

DODECAHEDRAL CAKE MOULDS.

With Tubes.

No.	317	327	347	367
Quarts	$1\frac{1}{2}$	2	3	4
Inches	$7\frac{1}{2}$x2	$8\frac{1}{2}$x2	$9\frac{1}{2}$x$2\frac{3}{8}$	$10\frac{3}{4}$x$2\frac{1}{2}$
Per doz	5.25	6.00	7.50	9.00
Each				

"Case Lots," 6 doz. of a size.

DODECAHEDRAL CAKE MOULDS.

With Tubes.

No.	1720	1730	1740	1750	1760
Quarts	2	3	4	5	6
Inches	$8\frac{1}{2}$x$2\frac{7}{8}$	$9\frac{1}{4}$x$3\frac{1}{8}$	$9\frac{3}{4}$x$3\frac{1}{4}$	$10\frac{1}{4}$x$3\frac{1}{2}$	$11\frac{1}{2}$x$3\frac{3}{4}$
Per doz	7.50	9.00	10.50	12.00	13.50
Each					

"Case Lots," 6 doz. of a size.

TURK'S HEAD CAKE MOULDS.

No.	61	$61\frac{1}{2}$	62	63	64
Quarts	$1\frac{1}{2}$	2	3	4	6
Inches	$7\frac{1}{4}$x$3\frac{3}{8}$	8x$3\frac{3}{4}$	$8\frac{1}{2}$x$3\frac{3}{4}$	$9\frac{1}{2}$x$3\frac{7}{8}$	11x$4\frac{1}{2}$
Per doz	7.50	9.00	10.50	12.00	15.00
Each					

"Case Lots," 3 doz. of a size.

From Iron Clad Manufacturing Co. Catalog, Jan. 1890

Several companies produced graniteware, most firms identifying their products by a paper label glued to the item. The St. Louis Stamping Company of St. Louis, Missouri, used a paper label picturing their trademark, consisting of the words "Patent Granite Iron Ware" and the illustration of a graniteware pot. This company patented their graniteware May 30, 1876. Lalance & Grosjean of New York, Chicago, and Boston, used a paper label in later years, but earlier pieces had "L & G" burnt into the enamel. The Iron Clad Manufacturing Company of 22 Cliff Street, New York, patented its graniteware in 1884; the paper label bore the company's initials, "I. C. M. Co.".

Manufacturers in the early 1900s were the Lisk Manufacturing Company and the National Enameling & Stamping Company. The latter firm used a paper label stating "Nesco Royal Granite Enameled Ware," and "Nescoware is everywhere." In the 1920s The Republic Stamping & Enameling Company of Canton, Ohio, also used a paper identifying label; it bore a lion trademark and the words, "Old English Gray Ware." Gray was the most common color in graniteware but it was also made in mottled light blue, dark blue, black, green, turquoise, and a brown called onyx. Most of the solid white pieces with a blue edging were made after the turn of the century.

From McClure's Magazine, Feb. 1900

Hornware

Horn beaker, circa 1800.
*Courtesy Henry Francis
du Pont Winterthur
Museum*

Hornware was common in the seventeenth and eighteenth centuries in America and even earlier in Europe. Such primitive North American peoples as the Eskimos and the Indians made ladles and spoons of horn, the Eskimos using the horns of the musk ox. Horns for blowing were fashioned in biblical times.

The gelatine in animal horn makes it an easy material to cut and mold when it is softened by heat. The horns of the ox were most used in the making of old hornware items, but those of the cow, bison, buffalo, sheep, goat, and antelope were also used. The tips of the horns, which are solid, were sawed off to be used in the making of handles for umbrellas, knives, forks, and wax sealers and to be cut into buttons.

Some horns have a bony core which was first removed by soaking the horns in water for five or six weeks. The hollow part of the horn was then softened by soaking it in boiling water for about half an hour. The horn was next slit with a sharp, pointed knife, spread out flat, and pressed between heavy, heated and greased iron plates. After being sufficiently pressed, the sheets of horn could be separated quite easily into thin layers. Pieces of these slices were used in old-time lanterns in place of glass, hence the word "lanthorn." Occasionally even small house windows, especially those with diamond panes, were fitted with sheets of horn instead of glass. Watch-face covers were also made of slivers of horn. It is a nonshatterable and semitransparent material.

Horn was easily stained to resemble tortoise shell and could scarcely be distinguished from it. The horn was colored reddish-brown and was left streaked and spotted. Then it was made into snuff boxes, pill boxes, fancy hair combs, lockets, straight-

razor handles, shoehorns, spectacle rims, and decorative medallions.

Horn scoop, circa 1750.
*Courtesy Colonial
Williamsburg*

When heated, the horn sheets could be molded
into almost any shape which would be retained
as the horn cooled. The articles were then polished
with rottenstone and oil, the fine patina of the
finished horn items giving them a most handsome
appearance. The parings, scrapings, and other
little pieces of horn were collected, softened, and
pressed into different forms. Drinking vessels and
gunpowder containers were often scratch-carved,
a type of decoration called "scrimshaw" which
was used on ivory and bone as well. Plates, bowls,
tumblers, saltcellers, sugar bowls with lids, and
napkin rings were practical kitchen items. Apoth-
ecary scoops for the druggist and pie crimpers for
the cook were molded of thin horn. Plain and
fancy horn spoons, knives, and forks were made,
some with applied decorative silver shields. Large
ladles were both attractive and useful. Beakers,
tumblers, and goblets were various types of drinking vessels formed of horn.

Hornbooks, the forerunners of today's primers,
were used in the days before printing was common.
A hornbook consisted of a single leaf, handwritten
on parchment or lettered on vellum, illustrating
the small and capital letters of the alphabet, the

Lord's Prayer, and, in addition sometimes, the vowels, diphthongs, and the Arabic and Roman numerals. The hornbooks were a matter of individual creation, and hence their writings varied. The leaf was placed on a wooden paddle and covered with a transparent sheet of horn to protect it. Then page and horn were tacked to the paddle with little hand-wrought nails. These crude early textbooks were commonplace items before 1760, some still being made as late as 1850, yet few original copies now exist.

There was little work for the hornsmith, as was also true of the wireworker and the tinsmith, after the passing of the Gay Nineties. Most horn items produced today are manufactured in Europe and are purely ornamental and frivolous. Gone are the days when one needed a beaker and made it himself of horn because the horn was handy and free.

Ladle made of musk-ox horn and a horn spoon. *Courtesy Imperial Oil Ltd.; C. W. Jefferys Imperial Oil Collection*

Ice has been used for many years to preserve food; it is said that ice was taken from Alpine regions to ancient Rome. In the eighteenth century, blocks of natural ice were cut by handsaws from lakes, ponds, and rivers, taken to the specially constructed storage places or icehouses on the individual homestead, and there covered with straw or sawdust to insulate it. The icehouses were usually constructed of wood and were windowless.

In the 1800s the ice trade was of great importance, and ice was harvested on an enormous scale. Horse-drawn snowplanes or scrapers removed the snow from the ice, on which ice plows then cut deep grooves to mark off large squares. The first few blocks were cut out by hand, but the remainder could then be easily split off with an ice spade forced into the grooves. The ice cakes were floated in channels to the banks of the pond

Ice Accessories

Ice shaver, steel shaver on iron base, circa 1860. *Courtesy Colonial Williamsburg*

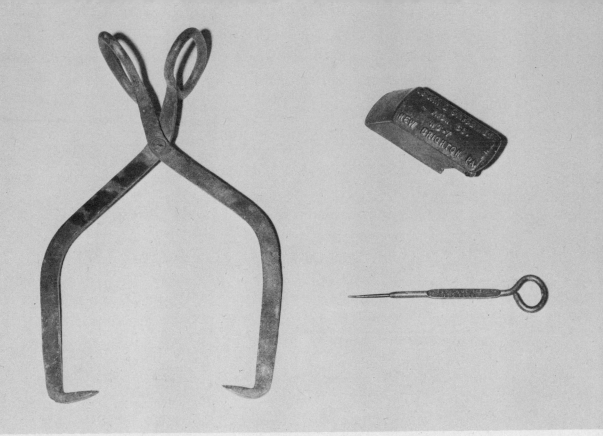

Left: Hand-wrought iron ice tongs. *Right, top:* Cast-iron ice shaver marked "Logan & Strobridge Iron Co., New Brighton, Pa." *Right, bottom:* Cast-iron ice pick marked "Pick our ice, it's pure"

or river and stored in huge icehouses. Straw and sawdust were packed around the ice just as in the smaller individual icehouses. Ice was exported from the United States to Great Britain, the East and West Indies, and South America.

The manufacture of artificial ice began to be carried on extensively in the 1890s. Ice was delivered to the home for use in iceboxes or refrigerators, first by horse-drawn ice wagons and later by ice trucks. The iceman was a familiar neighborhood sight until as recently as the early 1940s. Hand-in-hand with the vanishing iceman have gone the accessories for his product—the tongs, the ice pick, the ice shaver, the ice chisel, and, of course, the icebox itself.

Many of these ice accessories bore the name of the ice company from which they were purchased or, as was often the case, from which they were provided gratis to their customers. Some of these

ICE PICKS

No. 202 7½ inches Long, Needle Point, Cocobolo Handles_____Per dozen $1.50

No. 2004 9½ inches Long, Needle Point, Heavy Tinned Cap _____Per dozen $1.50

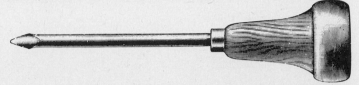

No. 1002 8¾ inches Long, Heavy Tinned Cap_____Per dozen $2.00

No. 903 Sliding Pick, 7 inch Steel Awl, Heavy Japanned Head _____Per dozen $2.00

All the above, half dozen in a Box.

"HURWOOD" ICE PICKS

A One-Piece Ice Pick. Needle Point, with Steel Extending through the Handle. The Point can neither be bent or broken in ordinary use. No chopping of ice necessary, just push the Pick through the Cake.

No. C Entire Length, 9½ inches; Blade, 5½ inches, 5/32 inch Steel, Ebonite Finish Handles ___Per dozen $3.30

No. A Entire Length, 9½ inches; Blade, 5½ inches, 7/32 inch Steel, Ebonite Finish Handles____Per dozen $3.60

No. D Entire Length, 9½ inches; Blade, 5½ inches, 7/32 inch Steel, Ebonite Finish Handles___Per dozen $4.75

To break the Ice in small pieces, use the Iron-Banded Head. The Hexagon form of Head prevents the Pick from rolling when laid down. Half dozen in a Box.

From Biddle Hardware Co. Catalog, 1910

ICE CHISELS

No. 387, 8 inches long, Steel Blades.

Ash Handles, Tinned Iron Bands___Per dozen $1.75

One dozen in a Box.

No. 1000, 10½ inches long, Polished Handles.

Per dozen _____ $3.50

Half dozen in a Box.

Entire Length, 41 inches.   Heavy Forged Steel Blade, 4½ inches wide.

No. **158** With Hickory Malleable D Handles _____Per dozen $14.00

"ENTERPRISE" ICE SHREDDERS

FOR SHAVING ICE COARSE OR FINE

NO. 23

Similar to the No. 33 and differs only in its being somewhat smaller, having no Lid and the Teeth part of the Bowl.

No. **23 Tinned**_____Per dozen $1.75

NO. 33 AND 34

No. **33 Tinned,**   Steel Blade___Per dozen $6.00
" **34 Nickel Plated,** "   " ___ "   "   18.00

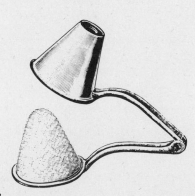

NO. 43

The No. 43 Shredder differs from the No. 33 only in shape and the Blade being placed in the Lid instead of bottom of Bowl. It is especially adapted for the use of venders selling "Snow Balls," as by hole in the small end of Cone the Ball can be readily flavored and easily ejected.

No. **43 Tinned**_____Per dozen $9.00

From Biddle Hardware Co. Catalog, 1910

ICE CHIPPERS AND SHAVES

CROWN ICE CHIPPERS

For Chipping Ice for use in Ice Cream Freezers or any purpose for which Cracked Ice may be needed.

Per dozen_____ $7.00

One dozen in a Case.

GEM ICE SHAVES

A Simple Handy Tool for Shaving and Collecting Ice from Blocks without removing latter from Ice Chest.

Per dozen_____ $7.00

One dozen in a Case.

CROWN ICE CHIPPER

GEM ICE SHAVE

ICE TONGS

STEEL HANDLE   **WOOD GRIP**

ELY'S DOUBLE JOINTED, STEEL, DIAMOND POINTS

WITH HEAVY FORGED STEEL HANDLES

No	12	15	18	1	3
To open, inches	12	15	18	20	24
Per dozen	$4.00	6.00	7.50	9.50	12.00

WITH STEEL HANDLES AND WOOD GRIP

No	24	28
To open, inches	24	28
Per dozen	$13.00	14.50

FAMILY

Tinned _____ Per dozen $2.50

One dozen in a Box.

From Biddle Hardware Co. Catalog, 1910

"advertising" ice tools bore "slick" slogans. One old ice pick stated "PICK OUR ICE/IT'S PURE." The reverse read "CHARLES WIS-KOW & SONS/PHONE GILMORE 0316," a Baltimore, Maryland, firm that has long been out of business.

Ice shavers usually carried the name of the ironworks which manufactured them, such as the Logan & Strobridge Iron Company, New Brighton, Pennsylvania. It is surprising how many shavers with diverse ironworks labels on them may be found.

Many ice tongs were hand-forged by the local blacksmith. These hand-forged tongs are doubly interesting because they represent both the vanishing blacksmith and the vanishing iceman.

Factory-made ice tongs came in many sizes— large, medium, and small, some of which folded even smaller. These, too, often bore the name of an ice company.

Ice chippers with saw-toothed blades were made both by blacksmiths and in factories. Some of the factory-made ones had wooden handles or a metal bottle opener opposite the chipping blade. These were also called ice chisels. Some had crucible-steel needle points for finer chipping.

The ice picks were usually steel awls with cherry, maple, or other hardwood handles; some had imitation cocobolo handles. Those with cast-iron handles had the advertising pressed into the metal, while the wooden ones had less-durable printed advertising.

Gas and electric refrigerators have largely replaced the icebox, and the iceman is almost non-existent in the cities of the United States today.

Ice cream, as we know it, was concocted in Europe over three hundred years ago. It was often called "frozen milk," "cream ice," or "ice milk." Settlers brought the formula for this delicious dish with them when they arrived in America. The first newspaper advertisement in the Colonies for ice cream appeared in the New York *Gazette* on May 10, 1777. George Washington mentioned an ice-cream machine in his account book in 1784, and the gracious Dolly Madison served ice cream to her distinguished guests during a party for the second inauguration of President James Madison (1813). Some of the oldest ice-cream freezers were attractive porcelain jars, with liners around which the ice and coarse rock salt were packed to freeze the cream; snow was sometimes used in place of ice.

However, most of the ice cream in the United States has always been commercially made. The first American patent for an ice-cream freezer was issued in 1848. By 1850 ice cream was being produced commercially at 180 Exeter Street in Baltimore by Jacob Fussell, and its manufacture proved to be a highly successful business.

Despite the ease of obtaining commercially made ice cream, the Victorian housewife dearly loved to make and serve this dessert at home. The

Ice-Cream Freezers

From Century Magazine,
July 1889

ICE CREAM FREEZERS.

Gooch's Big 4.

THE PEERLESS
Are the best. They are a little higher price than others, but are well worth the difference.

THE ZERO
is cheaper, not so good as Peerless, but better than any other Freezer in the market.

THE PET,
cheaper than Zero, and a very good one.

THE BOSS
are very low price. Anybody could afford to buy one. All are good, solid and well made.

MRS. SMITH.—I'm so glad I got the Peerless Freezer, for it makes the Cream so nice, I am proud of it; besides, it takes so little ice, I hardly miss it from the refrigerator. My old freezer was not half as good.

MRS. BROWN.—Well, I must get one, for I have heard several speak of them as being better than any others, and they say they are just as cheap.

———

Sold by leading dealers EVERYWHERE.

THE GOOCH FREEZER CO. Cincinnati, Ohio.

Easy to turn - even for little hands

YOUR children—just as easily as you—can now freeze ice cream in the easy-turning, 5-minute, gearless ACME Freezer, and share with you the benefits of pure, wholesome, safe ice cream made at home under ideal sanitary conditions.

Thorough churning by turning alone insures velvety texture. In the ACME Freezer, *the inner can revolves around a stationary dasher;* the contents are whipped thoroughly and quickly, and five minutes' easy turning results in ice cream of a delightfully smooth, velvety consistency—*any flavor.* The ACME Freezer also produces delicious water ices, sherbets, parfaits, mousses, etc., and saves ice. Recipe-folder FREE to every purchaser.

All-metal construction, and the elimination of gears insure unusual durability. Both the *special dollar* ACME, (*bright-galvanized,* 2-quart size); the beautiful, glossy 2-quart and 4-quart *enameled-galvanized* ACME Freezers; and the pint size—ACME Jr. (specially made for children, very small families and sick rooms), are built to give long, useful service.

ACME the 5 minute ice cream FREEZER
MANUFACTURED BY
ACME CAN CO. Inc.
PHILADELPHIA. PA.
U.S.A.

Endorsed by leading Home Economics teachers and sold by reputable hardware, housefurnishing and department stores *everywhere. Accept no imitations or substitutes.*

If your dealer cannot supply you, Use This Coupon—

ACME FREEZER
PRICES
2 qt. Enamel-Galvanized $1.50
4 qt.   "   " $2.50
2 qt. Bright   " $1.00
Acme Jr. pint size $.60

ACME *The Enameled Galvanized*
FIVE MINUTE FREEZER

ACME CAN COMPANY
Dept. L.J.6, Philadelphia, Pa.

Enclosed find $_____

for_____
        ACME ICE CREAM FREEZER

Name_____

Address_____

From Ladies' Home Journal, June 1925

slow, tedious job of cranking the freezer was often relegated to the youngsters with the promise that they could "lick the dasher."

Many different companies produced a variety of ice-cream freezers in the 1800s and early 1900s, each professing to be better than the other, and competition was keen. The Gooch Freezer Company of Cincinnati, Ohio, claimed its freezer used very little of the then-precious ice. The White Mountain Freezer Company of Nashua, New Hampshire, boasted that its freezer was warranted to freeze cream in one half the time of any other freezer in existence. With great confidence, the Shepard's Lightning Freezer, made at the Mammoth Foundry in Buffalo, New York, stated that its freezer made "the lightest, purest, and best ice cream that can be made."

The Lightning Freezer made by the North Brothers Manufacturing Company of Philadelphia, Pennsylvania, lured customers with a free booklet, *Freezers and Freezing*, by Mrs. S. T. Rorer. The White Mountain Freezer Company countered with a book of "practical receipts" compiled by Mrs. Mary J. Lincoln, author of *The Boston Cook Book*. The guarantee of "no danger from zinc poisoning" probably also boosted the sales of the extensively advertised White Mountain Freezer.

Though the advent of the ice-cream cone at the St. Louis World's Fair in 1904 increased the use of commercial ice cream, it did not dim the enthusiasm of the housewife for making ice cream at home. In the *Delineator* magazine for August, 1906, Isabel Gordon Curtis gave detailed directions, in a column called "The Progress of a Housewife," for making this frozen dessert at home. Violets from the garden, fresh bananas, rum, brandy, or nuts were added to the ice cream for flavor.

From Biddle Hardware Co. Catalog, 1910

Cont'd on page 137

ROYAL ICE CREAM DISHER

ROYAL ICE CREAM DISHERS

Made in sizes No. 4, 5, 6, 8, 10, 12, 16 to Quart.
Bowls made of 3X Charcoal Plate. Handles of Heavy Double Tinned Wire. Cutters of Double Tinned Steel.

Per dozen -- $2.50

ICE CREAM FREEZERS

"ARCTIC"

Single Motion, Can revolves while Dasher remains Stationary. Double Self-Adjusting Wood Scrapers, White Pine Pail, Flat Galvanized Iron Hoops, Can, Tin Plate.

Size, quarts	1	2	3	4	6	8	10	12	15
Each	$2.20	2.60	3.00	3.60	4.60	5.90	7.60	9.00	10.40

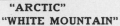

"ARCTIC"

"WHITE MOUNTAIN"

Triple Motion, Can revolves in one direction, Outside Dasher moves in opposite direction, Inside Dasher moves in opposite direction to Outside Dasher, Double Self-Adjusting Wood Scrapers, Second Growth White Pine Pail, Flat Galvanized Iron Hoops, Can, Best Tin Plate.

Size, quarts	1	2	3	4	6	8
Each	$2.50	3.20	3.80	4.40	5.60	7.20
Fly Wheels only		1.20	1.20	1.20	1.80	2.00

Size, quarts	10	12	15	20	25
Each	$9.30	11.70	14.00	18.00	23.20
Fly Wheels only	2.80	4.40	4.40	5.20	6.40

"WHITE MOUNTAIN"

"FREZO"

One Motion, Full Size Tubs and Cans, Best Quality Lumber, Best Coated Tin Plate, Improved Dasher with Double Scrapers. Same style as Dana Freezer.

Size, quarts	1	2	3	4	6	8	10	12
Each	$2.20	2.60	3.00	3.60	4.60	5.90	7.60	9.00

"FREZO"

From Biddle Hardware Co. Catalog, 1910

ICE CREAM FREEZERS

"AMERICAN TWIN"

Freezes Two Flavors of Ice Cream or an Ice or Sherbet and Ice Cream at One and the Same Time, in One Freezer.

The Can is divided in Two Parts by a Vertical Partition. One flavor is placed in one, the other in opposite side of Can, in each of which the Scrapers, etc., operate. The Can cannot be turned as in old style Freezers, because of the Partition. It is therefore swung to and fro by a rocking motion of the Crank. This is a more comfortable and much easier movement, and very much less tiresome than turning a Crank.

Cedar Pails with Electric Welded Wire Hoops, all Inside Parts Tinned, Outside Parts Galvanized.

Size, quarts	2	3	4	6	8
Each	$3.50	4.10	5.00	6.40	8.00

Size, quarts	10	12	15	20
Each	$10.00	12.00	16.00	20.00

FREEZERS FOR RESTAURANTS, HOTELS, BOARDING HOUSES, CONFECTIONERS, ETC.

WITH CRANK

"Crown"	8 qt.	$10.00
"	10 "	12.00
"	14 "	14.00
"	18 "	19.00
"	24 "	23.00
"Jumbo Lightning"	20 "	19.00

WITH FLY-WHEEL

"Crown"	8 qt.	$14.00
"	10 "	16.00
"	14 "	18.00
"	18 "	24.00
"	24 "	29.00
"	32 "	34.00
"Jumbo Lightning"	14 "	17.00
" "	20 "	24.00

WITH PULLEY

"Crown"	14 qt.	$23.00
"	18 "	28.00
"	24 "	35.00
"	32 "	40.00
"Jumbo Lightning"	14 "	22.00
" "	20 "	28.00

The Crown Freezer is the same in construction as the Gem, the Jumbo Lightning as the Lightning, but made heavier and stronger.

From Biddle Hardware Co. Catalog, 1910

ICE CREAM FREEZERS

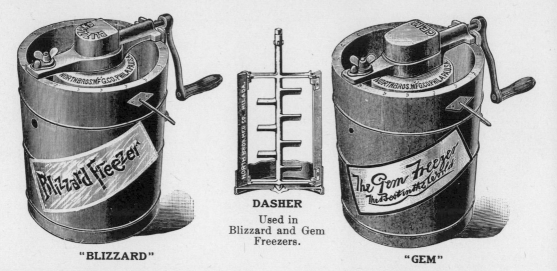

"BLIZZARD"

DASHER
Used in
Blizzard and Gem
Freezers.

"GEM"

"Blizzard," Single Action, Can revolves while the Dasher is held in the Cross Bar or Top Plate. The Cross Bar is not hinged, but similar to that of the Gem Freezer, and has the same fastening. The Dasher is same as that in the Gem Freezer, and has Automatic Twin Scrapers. White Cedar Pails with Electric Welded Wire Hoops. All Inside Parts Tinned, Outside Parts Galvanized.

"Gem," Double Action. Can and Dasher revolve in opposite directions. Cross Bar is not hinged, but is more readily removed and replaced. Automatic Twin Scrapers. White Cedar Pails, with Electric Welded Wire Hoops. All Inside Parts Tinned, Outside Parts Galvanized.

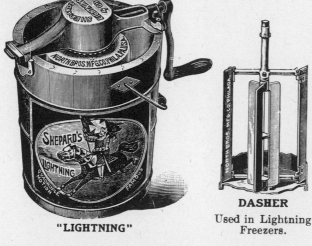

"LIGHTNING"

DASHER
Used in Lightning
Freezers.

"LIGHTNING"

Wheel Dasher. Quadruple Motion. Automatic Twin Scrapers. Top Plate Swings up as if hinged to Pail, but is Detachable. White Cedar Pails with Electric Welded Wire Hoops. All Inside Parts Tinned, Outside Parts Galvanized.

FLY WHEELS ONLY

For "Blizzard," "Gem" and "Lightning" Freezers.

For Freezers.		Diameter, inches.	Shaft, inches.	Weight, pounds.	Each.
2-3-4	All Styles	12	$7/16$	6	$1.20
6	" "	13	$1/2$	$8\frac{1}{4}$	1.60
8	" "	14	$1/2$	$10\frac{3}{4}$	2.10
10-12	" "	15	$9/16$	15	3.00
14	Gem & Blizzard	18	$9/16$	$21\frac{3}{4}$	4.10
14	Lightning	18	$5/8$	$21\frac{3}{4}$	4.10

Size, Quarts	1	2	3	4	6	8	10	12	14
"Blizzard" Each	$2.20	2.60	3.00	3.60	4.60	5.90	7.60	9.00	10.40
"Gem" "	2.40	2.80	3.30	4.00	5.10	6.50	8.40	10.00	11.50
"Lightning" "	2.40	2.80	3.30	4.00	5.10	6.50	8.40	10.00	11.50

From Biddle Hardware Co. Catalog, 1910

ICE CREAM FREEZERS

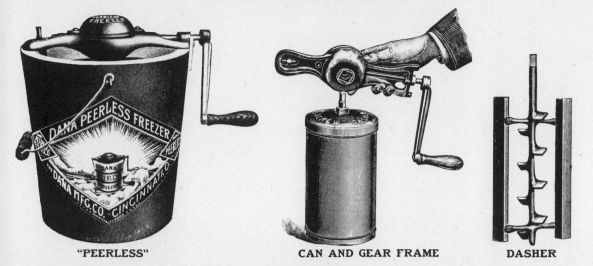

"PEERLESS"	CAN AND GEAR FRAME	DASHER

One Motion. Can revolves while Dasher remains stationary. No Grease on Can Top. All Gears enclosed separate from Freezing Apparatus in Detachable Top Plate. Best Quality Pails. All Inside Parts Tinned, Outside Parts Galvanized.

Size, quarts	1	2	3	4	6	8	10	12	16	20	25
"Peerless"	Each $2.50	3.20	3.80	4.40	5.60	7.20	9.30	11.70	15.00	18.00	23.20
Fly Wheels only	"		1.50	1.50	1.50	1.50	3.00	3.00	3.00	5.00	5.00	6.50

From Biddle Hardware Co. Catalog, 1910

From Century Magazine, Apr. 1888

From Good Housekeeping, July 1923

Cone-shaped ice-cream dishers or dippers were made of seamless tinned steel with steel or German silver knives which were revolved by turning the top knob. This action cut the ice cream loose from the dipper. The numbers on the dishers designated the number of dips to the quart. Later dippers were nickel-plated and worked by squeezing the handle, which in turn rotated the blades inside and released the ice cream. Dippers were also made in aluminum.

Indurated Fibre Ware

Indurated Fibre Ware experienced a brief popularity toward the end of the nineteenth century. This seamless ware was molded in one piece from wood pulp; the material was chemically treated to give it greater strength and durability. Since wood is a nonconducting material, the outer surface of articles made of this ware stayed cool even when the containers were filled with the hottest liquid. Hot or cold liquids retained their temperature for long periods in this ware. Some factories did not apply a finish to the outside of these vessels; others offered the ware in a variety of enameled colors. Neither paint nor varnish was applied to the interior of these utensils so that no taste would be imparted to foods. This was an exceptionally lightweight product which was rustproof and unaffected by temperature extremes. There were no hoops to drop off, such as there were on the old wooden buckets and pails. At twenty-five cents to two dollars per article, they were inexpensive items.

Some of the articles made of Indurated Fibre Ware were pails, tubs, basins, water coolers with spigots, baby baths, chamber pots, milk pans,

From Iron Age, Jan. 9, 1890

138

INDURATED FIBRE WARE.

Chamber Pail.
Plain Color, 55 cts.
Assorted Colors, 65 cts.

Star Water Pail.
Plain Color, 25 cts.
Enameled in Colors, 40 cts.

Cuspidor.
Plain Fibre, 35, 40, 50 cts.
Nickel Top, 75 cts. 90 cts.,
$1.75.

Baby Bath, Oval.
19 in. long, 14 in. wide, 6 in. deep.
Plain Color, 75 cts.
Enameled in Colors, $1.00.

Slop Urn.
Plain fibre, 50 cts.
All White Urns,
85 cts.

Ice Water Jars.
Five Sizes, $1.15, $1.40, $1.65,
$1.75 and $2.00.

Keelers and Wash Tubs.
25 cts. to $1.30.

From Van Heusen-Charles Co. Catalog, 1898

INDURATED FIBRE WARE.

• • • • • • • SEAMLESS • • • • • • •

PAILS——— ———KEELERS

TUBS——— ———SPITTOONS

BASINS——— Umbrella Stands

Water Coolers— ———SLOP JARS

MILK PANS——— ———Etc., Etc.

No Hoops
to Rust
and
Drop Off.

Bottoms
cannot
Drop Out.

EVERY ARTICLE WARRANTED.

MOULDED in one piece from wood pulp. Treated chemically, giving great strength and durability, and at same time making the ware IMPERVIOUS to liquids, hot or cold. Being neither painted nor varnished, it will not impart taste to anything put in it, and will not further absorb liquid or odor so as to become heavier or foul. Is very light. Has no hoops to drop or rust off. Warranted absolutely seamless and unaffected by extremes of weather.

Ask your grocer or hardware dealer to show you these goods. If he does not keep them send us his name.

PORTLAND, ME.
WATERTOWN, MASS. } FACTORIES: { OSWEGO, N. Y.
MECHANICVILLE, N. Y. LOCKPORT, N. Y.
WINONA, MINN.

UNION INDURATED FIBRE CO.,

General Office } 110 Chambers St., New York.   39 Wabash Ave., Chicago.

spittoons, cuspidors, slop urns, washtubs, umbrella stands, and keelers (shallow tubs). Factories in New York, Massachusetts, Maine, and Minnesota manufactured this ware. However, articles made of this wood pulp proved to be not as durable as anticipated, for they were easily crushed. Few pieces may be found intact today.

From Van Heusen-Charles Co. Catalog, 1898

**FIBRE WASH BOWL
AND PITCHER.**
Plain, 60 cts.

Ironing Boards

Before the invention of the folding ironing board as we know it today, clothes and linens were ironed on the broad, wooden kitchen table. Then what might truly be called ironing boards were devised. These boards did not have legs, but were supported by the kitchen table on one end and a kitchen chair at the other. They made the ironing of anything which had to be slipped over the board very troublesome. They were usually advertised as "well seasoned and will not warp or crack." The housewives tried to store their ironing boards flat, as many were not made of seasoned wood and warped easily. They also turned the boards occasionally so as to iron evenly on both sides, another precaution against warping. They were padded with an old blanket or something similar tacked to them and covered with muslin.

These ironing boards came in lengths varying from three to six feet. The shorter boards were called shirt boards or bosom boards, and upon these the stiffly starched shirt bosoms were pressed.

The longest boards were for ironing the fashionable full-length skirts of the day, sheets, and tablecloths. The skirt boards were usually about a foot longer than the longest skirts.

A sleeve board was a valuable ironing aid. It stood on its own base and was often homemade of pine, maple, or oak, covered with flannel, and outer-covered with muslin. A sleeve board was made slightly narrower than the average sleeve so it could be slipped on and off and turned around the board easily. The board was usually made about one inch thick so it could be turned on edge to permit the ironing of the backs of sleeves without pressing in creases. The Acme Sleeve Board, patented in 1899, was attached to the ironing board with an iron clamp. It was manufactured by

From Van Heusen-Charles Co. Catalog, 1898

IRONING BOARD.
On Folding Stand.
Can be adjusted to three different heights.
$1.00.

C. H. Smith & Co., 12 Federal Street, Boston, Massachusetts.

A variety of boards was considered essential to a convenient laundry outfit.

The first folding ironing boards in the nineteenth century were actually folding ironing tables. These were made of white pine and had a lidded compartment underneath to store the irons, beeswax, ironing stands, and the blankets used to pad the table for ironing. These resemble the old hutch tables and are sometimes mistaken for them and consequently attributed to be much older than they really are.

From Building with Assurance, Morgan Woodwork Organization, 1921

SLEEVE BOARDS.
Made of well-seasoned woods.   25 cts. to 85 cts.

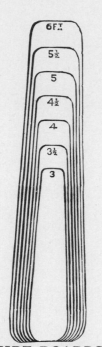

6 F.T.
5½
5
4½
4
3½
3

SHIRT BOARDS.
seasoned and will not warp or crack.
50 to 85 cts.

FOLDING IRONING TABLES.
$3.50 to $6.00.
Made of the best White Pine and have an apartment
for holding irons, blankets, etc.

*From Van Heusen-
Charles Co. Catalog, 1898*

In the nineteenth century it was considered a mark of cultivated fastidiousness to have one's linen shirts and other linen items show more luster than could be imparted by only a vigorous ironing. Hence, for a more glistening surface, a little gumarabic water was mixed with the starch. A couple of ounces of the gum, dissolved in boiling water, strained, and bottled, supplied the laundry for several weeks. A tablespoon of the solution was sufficient for a quart of starch. This made an excellent stiffening for laces and sheer muslin as well as linens.

Folding ironing boards similar to those in use today, but made all of wood, were widely used by 1905. This convenient household article was in great favor. One sold by Sears, Roebuck, and Company had a basswood top and hardwood legs which adjusted to three different heights.

About 1920 woodworking companies, such as Curtis Woodwork and Morgan Woodwork Organization, made the first folding ironing boards in wall cases. These were permanent installations. The ironing board dropped into rigid position from a storage cabinet built flat into the wall.

Juice Extractors

The lemon and lime, natives of Burma and India, seem to have been unknown to the ancient Greeks and Romans. However, they were widely used in Europe from the year 1200, and mechanical means for extracting their tangy juice probably were first contrived at that time. As a preventive against scurvy, the lemon and lime were considered essential foodstuffs on merchant ships during the 1800s. An English sailor was called a "limey" because of the old British rule that limes must be carried on ships for this purpose.

Sweet oranges, natives of China and Indochina, have been eaten in those countries since 2200 B.C. and in European countries since the fifteenth century. Orange groves were planted in St. Augustine, Florida, when it was settled in 1565 and in the mission at San Diego, California, in 1769. Later in the 1700s thick, wild orange groves, probably descendants of those originally planted, grew in Florida, and the fruit was eaten by the Seminole Indians. Historic Monticello, Thomas Jefferson's plantation in Charlottesville, Virginia, and Hampton, one of the great Georgian houses of America, near Towson, Maryland, had orangeries in the 1700s. In the early 1900s oranges were still a luxury, and children often found an orange tucked in the toe of their Christmas stocking. The grapefruit, a mutation of the shaddock, was first planted in this country in Florida in 1840.

The earliest juice extractors were probably of the reamer type. Those known in this country rather resembled a small potato masher with a corrugated head. In early New England the reamer-juicer was commonly made of maple or beech; finer ones, usually European-made, had wooden handles and china heads.

The manual reamer-juicer was gradually devel-

146

oped into the mechanical extractor consisting of two hinged sections made of wood or later of iron. The head and cup of the wooden models were sometimes also of wood. Lignum vitae, being very hard, was often considered the best wood to use for this part of the juicer. Although quite a few of this type of juicer were made at home, they were also produced in factories at a later date. Eventually, tinned, cast white metal, or white ironstone heads were used in these wooden juicers. Sometimes this simple wooden extractor was elevated on a wooden stand, allowing for better leverage, with the bowl or tumbler for catching the juices placed underneath the stand. In the 1880s a similar squeezer on a stand, marked "Acme," was available in iron. During the same period, there

Juice extractors. *Top, left to right:* Hinged wood, lignum vitae head; iron with wooden presser, marked "Pearl"; hinged wood with ironstone head. *Bottom, left to right:* Tinned iron with corrugated head; cast iron with plain head, marked "Boss." *Willafred Studios*

was a very robust iron clamp-on-the-table model with a cast-aluminum cup marked "Quick and Easy."

The Victorian era saw the development of many patented extractors. During this period there were numerous varieties of hinged juicers made completely of tinned cast iron. Some had plain cups; others had fluted ones. A patented model marked "Williams" had a hinged japanned cast-iron frame and a glass head. There was also a cast-iron one, marked "Pearl," with a hardwood head.

Easley's patents of July 10, 1888, and 1900 were juicers made entirely of glass with a fluted-cone projection on a saucerlike base, or, in some models, on a cone-shaped high base. These were similar to today's inexpensive manual extractors in which

Juice extractors. *Top, left to right:* Hinged iron frame, white metal cup parts, marked "Yankee Lidon"; hinged cast iron, marked "Williams," glass insert, circa 1898. *Bottom, left to right:* Glass, marked "Easley's patent, 1900"; glass, marked "Easley's patent, July 10, 1888." *Willafred Studios*

LEMON SQUEEZERS

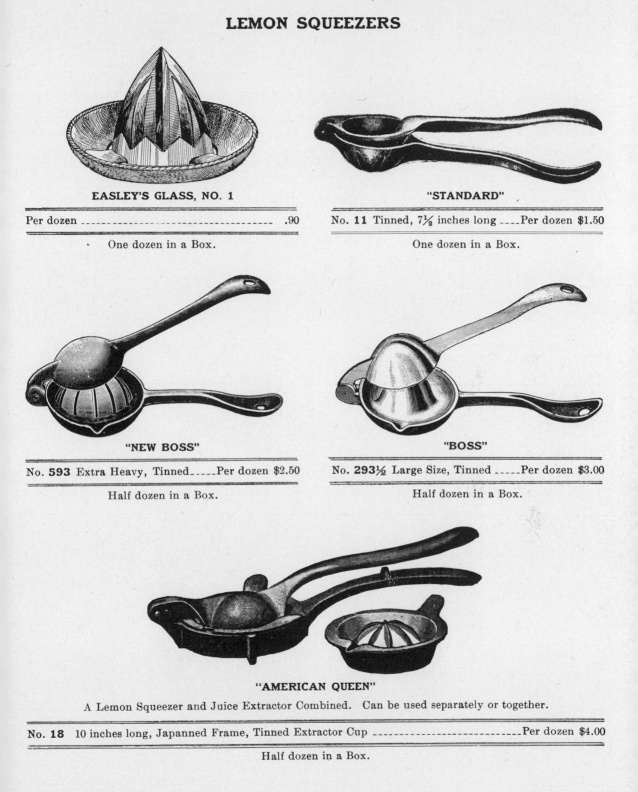

EASLEY'S GLASS, NO. 1

Per dozen _____ .90

One dozen in a Box.

"STANDARD"

No. 11 Tinned, 7½ inches long ____Per dozen $1.50

One dozen in a Box.

"NEW BOSS"

No. 593 Extra Heavy, Tinned_____Per dozen $2.50

Half dozen in a Box.

"BOSS"

No. 293½ Large Size, Tinned _____Per dozen $3.00

Half dozen in a Box.

"AMERICAN QUEEN"

A Lemon Squeezer and Juice Extractor Combined.   Can be used separately or together.

No. 18   10 inches long, Japanned Frame, Tinned Extractor Cup _____Per dozen $4.00

Half dozen in a Box.

From Biddle Hardware Co. Catalog, 1910

the hand is the main working part. Elegant old porcelain two-part lemon squeezers are most likely of European origin; the majority probably are French. Some of these are delicately and artistically hand painted.

A polytypic collection of old juice extractors would include iron, wood, glass, and china items in the reamer and in the hinged types. The rarer elevated and clamp-on designs would be necessary to really call the collection complete. An interesting adjunct to such a collection would be a lemon razor. This kitchen tool was used to slice thin sections from lemons and oranges for flavoring drinks and for the making of candied peel and marmalades.

From Van Heusen-Charles Co. Catalog, 1898

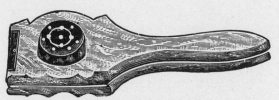

HARD WOOD LEMON SQUEEZER.

With Lignumvitæ cup and ball and nickel hinges.   75 cts.

Mashers have been used for the preparation of food for centuries, and no old-time American kitchen was complete without a variety of them.

The eighteenth-century kitchen had huge mashers for tamping the cabbage for sauerkraut, smaller ones for mashing potatoes and vegetables, and very small ones for mashing, grinding, and powdering spices and herbs. These were made of common maple, lovely grained bird's-eye and curly maple, deep brown walnut, or magnificent red lignum vitae, a hard, heavy wood. The smallest mashers, although especially made for the preparing of herbs and spices, were also suited to the preparation of small portions of vegetables for the very young, the ill, and the elderly.

The medium-sized all-wooden mashers were quite common throughout the eighteenth and nineteenth centuries. These were made of hardwood and show the marks of years of continual hard usage. Some of these had a companion piece with a handle in the same pattern but with a meat tenderizer head in place of the masher head. Squat, thick mashers with a large, flat head were actually butter tamps used to force the butter tightly into the old butter tubs. Starkly plain mashers are often called Shaker mashers because their simple utilitarian shape is similar to the bold, clean lines of all Shaker furnishings. A more rare type of masher had the regular-sized masher head on one end and a smaller head on the other end, making it of dual purpose. Mid-nineteenth-century cookbooks often refer to these wooden mashers as "potato beetles," "beetle" meaning to "beat or ram." It is possible to build a large collection of these medium-sized mashers without repeating a single handle design.

Mashers, Tampers, and Toddy Sticks

Potato mashers with wooden handles and wire heads were the standard from about 1850 on. One with a heavy, retinned-wire twisted shank and a hardwood handle was advertised at the turn of the century as "the best kitchen utensil ever used" and sold for about five cents. These wire mashers came with round or square heads. One wire masher was twisted in a manner similar to a coil spring and sort of bounced back from the potatoes, thus easing this chore. During this same period there were sturdy mashers made all of iron with circular cut-out heads. Some of these with the added feature of a bottle-opener handle were made circa 1914; many having advertising stamped on the handles. "Merry Christmas, Happy New Year" was the seasonal greeting impressed on one. Similar round iron heads were also mounted on wooden handles.

Giant mashers almost two feet long were used for tamping the cut cabbage in the barrel when making sauerkraut. A very old one is still in use by the author for its original purpose.

Left to right: Iron and wood potato masher; captive ring masher; tinplated masher

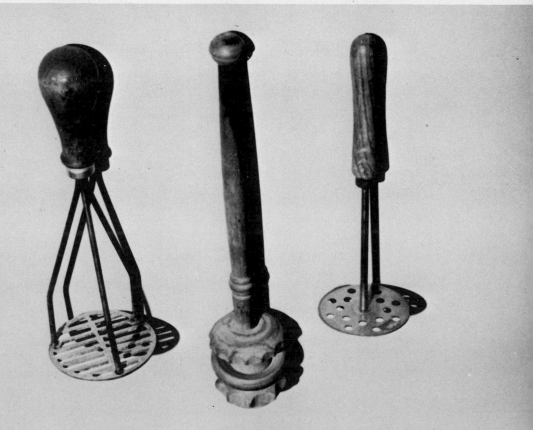

Toddy sticks, often confused with small mashers, were nicely turned little sticks used for stirring and crushing the sugar and lemon in the beverage called toddy. These sticks had small, flat heads, round ball-like heads, or, rarely, corrugated heads.

Pestles, separated from their mortars, sometimes served as mashers. Toddy sticks were likewise occasionally called upon to do duty as small mashers and grinders for herbs and spices.

Mahogany toddy stick, elaborately turned

Wooden mashers; large one at left is for tamping sauerkraut; handle of one at right may be used as a small masher

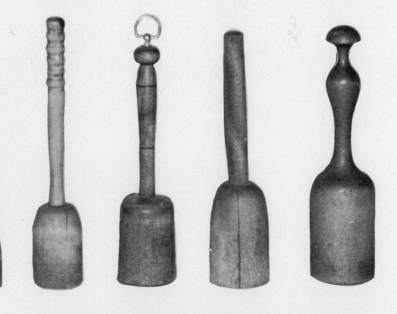

Mortars and Pestles

Hand-blown amber and green bottle-glass mortar and pestle, late eighteenth-century. *Courtesy National Gallery of Art*

Mortars and pestles were essential for grinding and crushing the spices and herbs so dearly prized by the early Americans. Coarse sugar, salt, spices, herbs, and soda were placed in the mortar and pounded and pulverized with the pestle. Mortars and pestles were known in biblical times. The American Indians and colonists pounded corn into samp (coarse hominy) in huge wooden mortars made of a hollowed tree stump or block of wood. Sometimes hollowed stone mortars were used, and the pestle was often a shaped stone. Mortars made from the burls on maple and ash trees withstood hard usage; lignum vitae and bird's-eye maple mortars and pestles were valued for their beauty as well as their durability.

A massive, heavy, blown-glass mortar and pestle was made in the late eighteenth century in New

154

Jersey. This mortar and pestle was made of clear window glass combined with amber bottle glass. Its form made it suitable for hard usage and attested to the versatility of the early American glassblower.

Apothecaries employed unglazed stoneware mortars and pestles to prepare their prescriptions. Josiah Spode II is known to have made these circa 1805. Pharmaceutical mortars were also made of marble, porphyry, and agate.

Later, mortars were carved of soapstone or cast in brass, bronze, or iron. The sizes and shapes of

Mortar and pestle made of stoneware in 1779 by Wedgwood and Bentley. *Courtesy Buten Museum of Wedgwood, Merion, Pa.*

No. 108 c.

Marble Mortars,
Four Sizes.

No. 96 a.
Mortars, Pine, Lignum-vitæ.
Also, Wedgewood Mortars, all sizes.

*From F. A. Walker &
Co. Catalog, 1886*

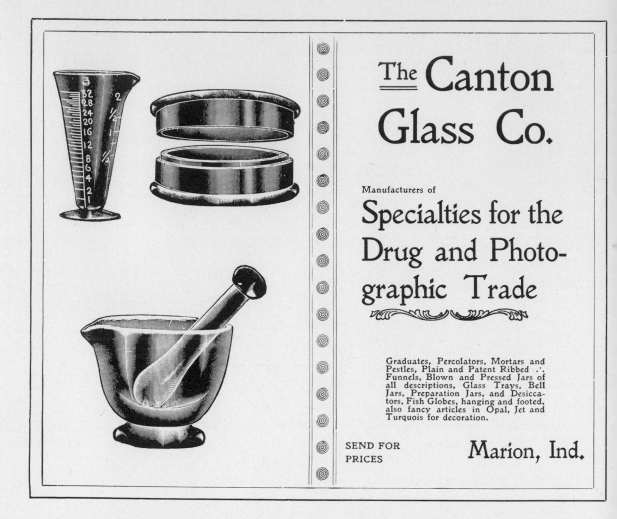

From Shepp's Photographs of the World, 1891

mortars were numerous. They ranged in height from three inches to three feet and in shape from bowllike to bell-form. The pestles were usually of the same material as the mortar although sometimes an appropriately sized animal bone served as a pestle.

A good mortar and pestle resisted scratching and did not stain. Mortars were, of necessity, strong vessels, and hence many old ones have survived for decades and even centuries.

The chief use of nickel was the plating of other metals, to which it gave a shiny, silverlike surface. The nickel-plating prevented the base metal from rusting and retained its silvery white sheen, as nickel does not oxidize or tarnish in the air.

Nickel was first discovered in 1751 and soon was found to be most suitable for plating other metals. Among early nickel-plated items were knives, forks, tea sets, buckles, horse bits, skates, surgical instruments, thermometer scales, chandeliers, gas fixtures, and the arms of railway seats.

The alloy called German silver or nickel silver was made up of one part of nickel, one part of zinc, and two parts of copper. It contained no silver at all. The best German silver was almost as white as pure silver and took a fine polish. It tarnished a greenish-yellow as compared to the black tarnish of sterling. Great quantities of forks, knives, spoons, and inexpensive jewelry were made of German silver in the nineteenth and early twentieth centuries.

Nickelware

NICKEL OMELET PAN.
$1.50.

NICKEL CALL BELL.

*From Van Heusen-
Charles Co. Catalog, 1898*

Nickel Chafing Dish Tray.
$1.00.

NICKEL PLATED DINNER
BELLS.

CHILD'S NICKEL TABLE TRAY.

NICKEL FLOUR DREDGE.

From Van Heusen-Charles Co. Catalog, 1898

The nontarnishing characteristic of nickel-plating made it ideal for kitchen utensils and tablewares since these articles were often exposed to the tarnish-producing elements of moisture and heat. The base metal most often used for these wares was brass or copper, or, for certain articles, steel. Serving trays, round and rectangular, were made in nickel-plate, often with elaborate scroll and floral designs embossed on their surface. Children's table trays had playful scenes on them, and

NICKEL OBLONG TRAYS.

25 cts. to $1.00.

NICKEL ROUND TRAYS

25 cts. to $1.00.

NICKEL BREAD TRAYS.

50 cts. to $2.00.

From Van Heusen-Charles Co. Catalog, 1898

German silver flatware, late nineteenth- and early twentieth-century patterns

bread trays were embossed "Bread." Chafing dish trays were round and of a simpler design. Call bells, in the days when one had a live-in servant to call, were nickeled. They were dome-shaped and were rung by tapping lightly on a push button with the finger. Wooden-handled nickeled dinner bells were made also.

Decorative holders for casserole dishes were manufactured in this silvery metal and provided an elegant appearance at a modest price. More utilitarian items were flour dredges, crumb tray and scraper or brush sets, egg boilers for the table, and wine coolers. Chafing dishes, round and oblong, were made for the cooking of oyster and hash dishes, Welsh rarebit, and venison. Russian coffeepots were an item with a unique appearance. Teakettles on stands over heaters were made in myriad shapes and designs. Some of these had the Argand central-draft burners which used a more efficient tubular wick as opposed to a flat wick. Nickel-plated nut bowls came equipped with an anvil and hammer. A cheese and cracker set consisted of a large engraved glass dish with a round, covered, nickel-plated cheese container in the center. A sixteen-inch plank for broiling meat or fish fitted into a pierced nickeled holder with end handles.

Most of this nickel-plated ware was made from the 1880s to about 1930. It was quite durable, and some pieces are still in active family service.

Russian Coffee Pots.

Brass, $3.00 to $5.50.
Nickel, $3.50 to $6.00.

From Van Heusen-Charles Co. Catalog, 1898

Nursing Bottles and Invalid Aids

The care of infants, the ill, and the invalid has been the duty of the housewife or homemaker for centuries. She is the guardian of the family health. Through the years, gadgets and devices have been invented in an attempt to simplify and perfect these duties.

Babies were seldom bottle fed in the eighteenth century. The oldest infant nursing bottles were made of tin. These rusted, often corroded, tin nursers look extremely unhygienic to us today, but they were the only mechanical nursers available to the eighteenth-century mother. They were entirely of tin, even the nipple; some had a handle and a push-on tight-fitting lid. These nursers are quite rare today and are difficult to find even in museum collections. An unusual model with two spouts is purported to have been contrived for the feeding of twins.

Baby bottles. *Left:* With rabbit design. *Right:* With scotty dogs design

162

The earliest glass nursing bottles were hand-blown or blown-in-the-mold and were usually of bubbly glass and flasklike in shape. Among nineteenth-century nursing bottles were the Millville, Baltimore, Empire, Acme, Sucker State, Screw-top, Home Nursing, Florence, and Barclay. The last six were flat oval bottles with upturned necks and round bottoms, used with a long rubber tubing and nipple. These could not be stood on end because of their round bases. Nursers from the 1920s and 1930s had small mouths and were delightfully embossed with rabbits, Scotty dogs, evergreen trees, and various nursery-type figures.

Small hardwood or japanned metal refrigerators were made in the mid-nineteenth century for use in the nursery or bedroom to keep baby's food and milk handy and cold. One, called the "Eddy Nursery Refrigerator," sold for $7.50 to $10.00.

Eighteenth-century tin nurser, hand-carved wooden nipple

White china invalid
feeder, unmarked.

"Cresolene Vaporizer,"
patented 1885

It held about one cubic foot of ice and was made by D. Eddy and Son of Boston. During this same period elaborate wicker baby baskets and bassinets were fashionable. These enchanting items were intricate and entrancing. An infant bath was made of tin and was held securely in position on its wooden stand by a strong elastic webbing.

Perforated tin nurse lamps came both plain and decorated with stenciled designs; some had attached snuffers. Less durable ones were made of china. They provided soft, muted light for the nursery or sickroom and were designed so that milk, a beverage, or gruel could be heated on

From Shepp's Photographs of the World, 1891

Eddy Nursery Re-
frigerator.

**INVALIDS' BLACK WALNUT
BACK REST.**

Baby Bassinetts.

*From Van Heusen-
Charles Co. Catalog, 1898*

them. Gruel was a thin porridge often used to nourish infants and the ill. A few nursery lamp-heaters came equipped with a removable little steam kettle which could be heated over the oil lamp or candle for use as a vaporizer. The "Vapo-Cresolene" lamp was a vaporizer patented in the late 1800s. It looked much like a miniature clear-glass oil lamp with a milk-glass hurricane shade. This lamp was fitted into a gilt iron frame with a tin cup and cover on top of the stand. Cresolene was put in the tin cup and heated by the kerosene

Unusual round blown-
glass nursing bottle.
*Courtesy Shelburne
Museum, Inc.; staff
photographer Einars J.
Mengis*

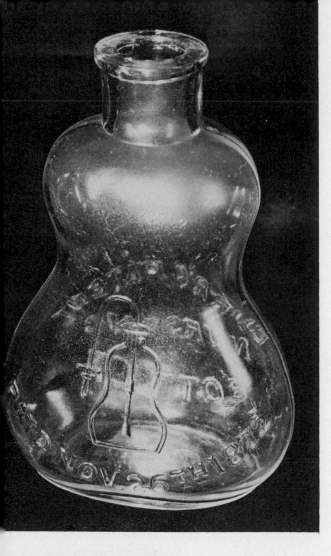

"Burr's Patent Nursing Bottle," patented Nov. 26, 1872. *Courtesy Shelburne Museum, Inc.; staff photographer Einars J. Mengis*

CHAMBERS.

	Rockingham.	Yellow.
No. 4..10-in...	.....	$4.25 doz.
No. 6.. 9-in...	$3.50	3.25 "
No. 9.. 8-in...	2.75	2.50 "
No. 12.. 7-in...	2.00	1.75 "

One-half added for Covers.

BED PANS.

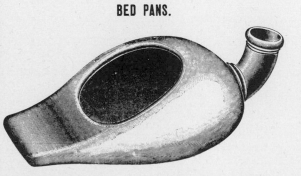

From Syracuse Stoneware Co. broadside of Aug. 15, 1896

	Rockingham.	Yellow.
o. 1..	$9.00	$8.00 per dozen

lamp beneath, thus creating vapors to ease coughs and colds. No doubt the little lamp alone sometimes served as a night light.

Many aids were created for the care of the bedridden. Plain, sturdy back rests for use in the bed were made of that now-rare wood, black walnut. Another type had a center section of caning. Both were adjustable for the patient's comfort.

From Shepp's Photographs of the World, 1891

Invalid feeders were teapotlike creations with a handle on one side and a long narrow spout on the other, the invalid or infant being fed through the tubular spout. These were made in plain white or decorated ironstone and china and in glass. These feeders were also called "feeding cups" and "papboats," "pap" being the name of a soft food for infants and invalids.

Nut trees are hardy and usually bear profusely; nuts keep well for a long period of time in a cool place and do not spoil quickly. These factors have made nuts a practical foodstuff in America ever since the continent was discovered. Nuts have been eaten as a dessert and used in the making of cakes, pies, soups, cookies, candy, and bread for centuries. They also have been made into a coffee substitute. The nuts most commonly used in the eighteenth and nineteenth centuries in America were almonds, English walnuts, black walnuts, acorns, hickory nuts, chestnuts, butternuts, chinquapins, beechnuts, and pecans. Some of these were native to American forests; others were imported. Acorns, eaten by the Indians and the colonists, are now considered poisonous and inedible.

Mallets and hammers probably served as the first crude nutcrackers. Cast-iron table model nutcrackers were made in the 1800s in the shapes of dogs, squirrels, and other animals. These worked by pressing a simple lever, usually the animal's

Nutcrackers

From Good House-keeping, Jan. 1921

"The Home Nutcracker,"
patented 1915

tail, which crushed the nut held in the animal's jaws. A brass nutcracker which was held in the hand had the jaw parts shaped like a rooster's head, the nut being held in the bird's beak. A nickel-plated, squeeze-handled steel nutcracker similar to modern ones bore the patent date 1889. One later variation of this type was marked "H.M.G. PAT. AUG. 10, 09" and another "PATENTED OCT. 22-19." Reproductions have been made of most of the animal-shaped nutcrackers.

A lever-operated nutcracker which clamped to the table was patented in 1916. It was marked "Home Nut Cracker, St. Louis, U.S.A." Another clamp-on type worked by turning a screw. It was

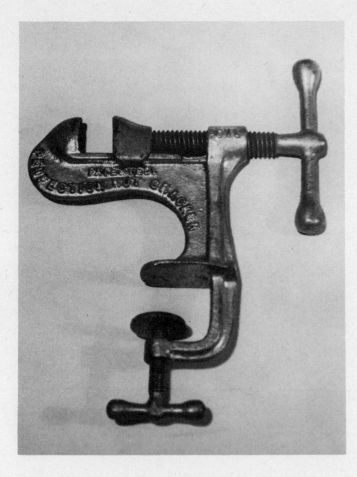

"Perfection" nutcracker

Nutcracker, patented Jan. 28, 1889. From Biddle Hardware Co. Catalog, 1910

QUACKENBUSH PLATED NUT PICKS AND CRACKS

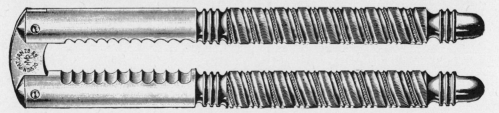

NO. 21 NUT CRACK

							Per dozen	
No. **22** Nickel Plated Nut Cracks, As in No. 122 Set							Per dozen $1.50	
" **0** " " " " " " " 80 "							" "	2.30
" **21** " " " " " " illustrated above							" "	3.00
" **20** " " " " " " in No. 40 Set							" "	5.00

Half dozen in a Box.

marked the "Perfection Nut Cracker" and was made in Branford, Connecticut, by the Malleable Iron Fittings Company. Similar to the Perfection was the "Hamilton Nut-Cracker." It was advertised as "one of the best on the market for pecans"; at one dollar it was worth a try. Another model of a twist-screw-type nutcracker was the Ideal nutcracker made by the Cook Electric Company of Chicago, Illinois, in the 1920s. It came in either plain nickel or highly polished.

Nuts are a protein-rich food used in some civilizations in place of meat. Properly stored, they may be kept for as long as two years. Nutcrackers made the task of procuring these nourishing kernels simpler and quicker.

Aluminum is the most modern of the common metals, the first practical method for producing aluminum having been devised by a Frenchman in 1844. This was a very expensive chemical method for separating aluminum from its ores. Despite the cost, commercial manufacturing began in 1854.

The first article made of aluminum was a toy rattle for the infant son of Napoleon III, the French emperor, in the 1850s. Napoleon also ordered aluminum forks and spoons for the use of his most honored guests. Aluminum was then more costly than silver or gold, but because of its lightness was considered valuable for many purposes. Napoleon III visualized how successfully such a strong, light metal could be used to lighten his army's equipment and thereby allow greater mobility. He ordered helmets, breastplates, and other articles of this new metal.

An alloy of two parts aluminum and one part silver was much used instead of silver for making drinking cups, candlesticks, spoons, forks, harness ornaments, telescopes, opera glasses, and specialized instruments.

The tip of the Washington Monument in Washington, D.C., placed on December 6, 1884, was made of aluminum. This was the first time many Americans saw this bright, untarnishing metal. This peak bore the Latin inscription, "Laus Deo" ("Praise to God"). During World War II, due to the scarcity of this metal, the aluminum peak was removed, melted, and used for plane production.

In 1886 the price of aluminum products dropped considerably when inexpensive electrical methods of production were initiated. The public was slow to accept the usefulness of aluminum at

Old Aluminum

The common teakettle helped start a metal, an industry, and a company on their way to success. The enthusiasm of a secretary at the sight of an aluminum teakettle led an early industrialist to add aluminum utensils to his product line. *A reenactment of the scene, from a motion picture. Courtesy of Alcoa*

Aluminum's ability to transfer heat quickly and evenly has made it ideal for cooking utensils since its earliest days. From the time Alcoa began its own line of cooking pots in 1901 to show their possibilities, the aluminum cooking utensil industry has grown to include many manufacturers and brands. First Wear-Ever ad, *Ladies' Home Journal,* Mar. 1902. *Courtesy of Alcoa*

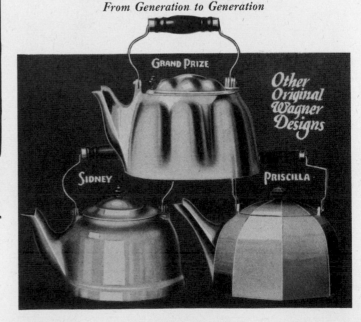

Aluminum "Stanley" flask, patented 1923

first, but it became popular in the 1890s, and its production increased rapidly thereafter.

Aluminum is much lighter in weight than most other metals and is one of the best conductors of heat. It is not greatly marred by oxidation, resists corrosion, and is nontoxic, which properties make aluminum a near-perfect material for cooking utensils. The earliest ware was made by pouring molten aluminum into molds, thus shaping it into thick-walled vessels with a pebbled texture called "cast aluminum." Aluminumware was also fabricated from thin sheets of the metal and called "stamped aluminum." The stamped aluminum heated quickly but did not retain the heat as well as the cast aluminum. After the turn of the century, pots, pans, coffeepots, kettles, double boilers,

.Always mention the HUNTER-TRADER-TRAPPER when writing to advertisers.

From Hunter—Trader—Trapper, 1919

Premium No. 230.   Aluminum Baking Set

Given Free for Seven Yearly Subscribers at
50 cents each, or Fourteen at 35 cents each

Given Free for Fourteen Counts

Here is a novelty which should interest all good housewives. Everyone knows how popular aluminum has become in the past few years for cooking utensils, and here is the set that just fills the bill. It consists of one baking pan 8¾ inches in diameter and 3 inches deep, one baking bowl 6½ inches by 2½ inches deep, one pie plate 9 inches by 1 inch deep, 1 pie plate 8 inches by 1 inch deep, and one jelly cake pan 9 inches by ½ inch deep. They are all made of pure aluminum, which is sufficient guarantee of their wear and general durability. We know of no one premium which represents more practical use, more excellent value on the terms offered than this aluminum set. The pans are light, are easily kept clean and are excellent for baking. Unquestionably aluminum kitchenware is needed by every housewife and we are pleased to be able to offer such a splendid set. We heartily recommend this set for your selection. Price, including one subscription to The Ladies' World, $2.10. Given free for **Fourteen** counts—see terms above. Price without subscription, $1.75. Receiver to pay express charges in any case.

From The Ladies' World, Dec. 1912

From Photographs of the World, 1891

The Aluminum Mfg. Co.

MANUFACTURERS OF

Aluminum Combs
and Fancy Goods, etc.

**TWO RIVERS
WISCONSIN**

colanders, egg separators, egg scales, and pastry jaggers were made of aluminum. Kitchenware made of aluminum is still being produced as a durable and efficient product.

Olive Stoners, Raisin Seeders, and Berry Hullers

Olives have been used since biblical days, and have been imported since early colonial times in America. They were either pickled or pressed into oil. Those to be pickled were harvested when green, soaked in strong lye or lime water, rinsed, and soaked in fresh water for several days. The lye or lime water softened the olives and made their taste less bitter. Finally, the olives were put into jars and covered with a strong, spicy brine of cinnamon, cloves, and other spices. The pickled olives also could be purchased in small wooden kegs.

The ripe olive was not canned in America until about 1901, when American canning experts discovered that the firm, dark, ripe olive could be canned successfully. The ripe olive, after being allowed to mature on the tree but not become soft ripe, is prepared for canning in much the same way as the green olive. Most of the ripe olives in our markets today are grown and packed in California. Both green and ripe olives are delicious and healthful foods.

A very useful olive stoner was worked by a strong push-knob controlled by a spring-encased shaft. This kitchen aid was sturdily constructed of metal. A very simple machine, it saved hours of frustrating work. An olive was placed on the stand, the plunger-type knob was pushed downward, and the stone was forced out through the opening in the stand, leaving only a small hole in the olive. The spring-loaded knob then returned to its original position. This was a nineteenth-century invention and did not require the dexterity and patience needed to seed an olive with a sharp knife.

Pounds of raisins went into the making of rich plum cake, raisins buns, Christmas pudding, and

Top: "Nip-It" strawberry huller, patented 1906. *Bottom:* "Boston Huller," patented 1894

Raisin seeder, patented 1891

No. 78a.
Olive-Stoner.
Very useful.

*From F. A. Walker & Co.
Catalog, 1886*

Olive forks, steel, circa
1914; one with round
head marked "Olive and
Pickle Fork"

mince pies. The Enterprise Raisin and Grape Seeder, simple in construction and easily adjusted, did its work rapidly and effectively. It worked by a crank handle and seeded grapes for preserving and cooking purposes. This contraption seeded raisins as fast as they could be dropped one at a time into the hopper. A smaller raisin seeder worked by a lever which pressed the raisins against a series of thick wires and thus forced out the seeds. Some raisin seeders warned in raised letters molded into the machine to "wet your raisins." The Gem, another cast-iron raisin seeder, was patented in 1895.

Berry hullers were little gadgets for removing the calyxes from certain fruits such as the strawberry and for plucking pin feathers from poultry. The "Boston Huller," patented in 1894, was made of nickel-plated brass. "The Nip-It Strawberry Huller," patented in 1906, was made of nickeled spring steel. These pincer-like devices are almost identical to modern strawberry hullers. The old ones, probably due to their small size, are difficult to find today. They were probably accidentally or purposely discarded years ago.

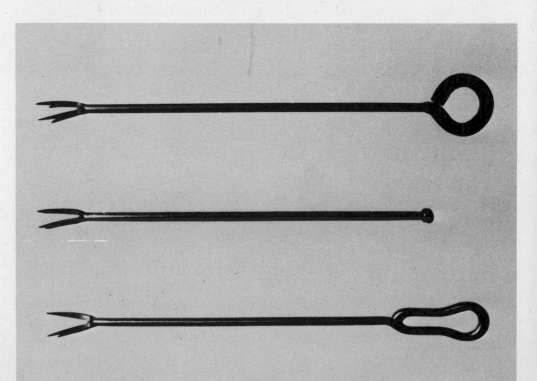

Pewter is an alloy of tin and copper or lead, sometimes with small quantities of antimony or zinc added. Fine old English pewter contained no lead. Pewter was known to the ancient Chinese, and relics of Roman pewter have been found in England. Old pewterware was made either by being poured into a mold, by being hammered into the desired shape over a form, or free-formed by being hammered into a shallow indentation in a block of wood.

In the eighteenth century all kinds of plates, dishes, mugs, bowls, teapots, coffeepots, marrow scoops, bedwarmers, sugars, creamers, pitchers, funnels, nursing bottles, inkwells, porringers, shakers, chalices, and even bedpans were made. Highly polished pewter pieces were kept on open display on the sideboard, just as fine silver was exhibited. Pewterware was useful and decorative as well, and had a gray, silvery sheen. Great quantities of it were produced between 1750 and 1850; and pewter largely replaced the earlier horn, leather, and wooden trenchers and beakers. However, its usage was confined to tableware, not cookware, as this soft metal has a low melting point.

Battered and broken pewter, especially spoons, were simply melted and recast. The brass molds in which the pewter was cast and recast were very expensive and much prized.

Eighteenth- and early nineteenth-century pewter had a sturdy shape and simple design and was quite heavy in weight. In the nineteenth century pewter was made into ale and beer mugs, syringes, beer pumps, inkstands, and plates for printing music. During this period pewter items were cast in iron or brass molds, and then finished on a turning lathe. Some were also made by hammer-

Pewter, Britannia, and Queen's Metal

183

Assortment of pewter items. *Courtesy Henry Francis du Pont Winterthur Museum*

ing out the metal, and some by the process of spinning.

Britannia metal was a kind of pewter and closely resembled it in color and appearance. Some called it a high-grade pewter, but it was thinner and lighter than older pewter. Britannia was made of tin and antimony with a little zinc, brass, copper, and, rarely, expensive bismuth. It was harder than the older pewter and slower to tarnish, and had a distinctive silvery-white color with a bluish tinge. When highly polished it was almost as white and handsome as silver. This

metal was used in the nineteenth century largely for the making of tea and coffee sets, trays, tureens, vegetable dishes, and candlesticks. Articles made of it were not cast but spun on the lathe or stamped. The shapes and designs of britannia were usually elaborate and often engraved. Britannia was also widely used after 1840 as a base for electroplated silverware.

Another type of pewter was called Queen's metal and was made into tableware, such as teapots and spoons, and used for plating harnesses, carriages, and furniture. It was composed mostly of tin with a little antimony, bismuth, copper, or lead, and a minute amount of zinc. It often contained no lead. Some considered it the finest pewter.

Old ice-cream molds were made of pewter. However, they were usually referred to as lead molds. This type of pewter consisted of a combination of about 61 per cent tin and 39 per cent lead. Most of these molds were used in commercial ice-cream plants, although some were sold for use in the home. These molds came in the shapes of fruits, vegetables, animals, ships, trains, and

Pewter bedpan. *Courtesy Henry Francis du Pont Winterthur Museum*

Pewter Santa Claus
ice-cream mold

patriotic designs. Some patriotic motifs were the eagle, American flag, American shield, and George Washington. The various forms of the eagle are the most sought after today. Six or eight individual molds could be made from a quart of ice cream. Only four or five companies manufactured ice-cream molds. Two leading ones marked their ware "E. & Co. N.Y." for Eppelsheim & Company and "S. & Co." for Scholl & Company. Those marked "C.C." were made in the nineteenth century in Paris, France.

From F. A. Walker & Co.
Catalog, 1886

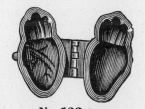

No. 122 c.   No. 123 c.   No. 124 c.

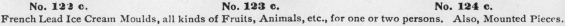

French Lead Ice Cream Moulds, all kinds of Fruits, Animals, etc., for one or two persons. Also, Mounted Pieces.

Early nineteenth-century pewter porringer made by Thomas Danforth Boardman and Sherman Boardman. *Courtesy The Metropolitan Museum of Art, Rogers Fund, 1909*

Pewter baby bottle, circa 1840; made by Thomas Danforth Boardman. *Courtesy The Metropolitan Museum of Art; gift of Joseph France, 1943*

During the Art Nouveau movement toward the end of the nineteenth century, pewter experienced a brief revival. This pewter was lighter in weight than the earlier pewter, and the shapes did not have the simple form of the older pieces. It was made purely for decorative rather than for utilitarian purposes.

The higher the tin content, the better the pewter; the higher the lead content, the poorer the pewter. More tin and less lead made the pewter brighter in appearance, more durable, and less likely to bend and dent; it also made it more expensive. But be it pewter, britannia, or Queen's metal, all have a soft, muted glow of inimitable charm.

The pie crimper was a simple device for cutting pastry, pie strips, and cookies, for fluting pie edges, and for sealing two pie crusts together. It was also sometimes called a "pastry jagger," a "pie trimmer," or a "pie sealer." Early nineteenth-century cookbooks often refer to this gadget as a jagging or gigling iron. Olden-day menus were rich with pies, not just the usual apple, peach, or pumpkin pie, but blue or red plum, dried apple, green gage plum, cranberry, rhubarb, whortleberry, gooseberry, green grape, and squash pies. So the crimpers saw a great deal of use.

Pie crimpers consisted of a fluted wheel attached to one end of a short handle for the dual purpose of fluting and cutting. Some had a wheel on one end and a curved serrated jagger on the other. Rarer ones had points opposite the wheel for pricking air holes in the pie crusts.

The earliest crimpers were of horn, wood, cast brass, iron, or whalebone, or a combination of these materials. There were also wooden-handled ones with porcelain wheels. Later ones were tin-plated and, in the early 1900s, some were patented with aluminum wheels.

The early bone or walrus ivory crimpers were often elaborately carved by sailors on the homeward voyages of a whaling vessel. Old wrought-iron ones were sometimes most attractively designed and decorated with hand chasing. One wrought-iron one had a quaint cut-out silhouette of a bird on one end; others had the initials of their creators on them. Some of these were presented by the makers to their sweethearts or were especially made for a new bride.

There was a great variety in the design and material of pie crimpers, a kitchen tool that is seldom used today.

Pie Crimpers and Pastry Jaggers

From Van Heusen-Charles Co. Catalog, 1898

PIE CRIMPER.

5 cts.

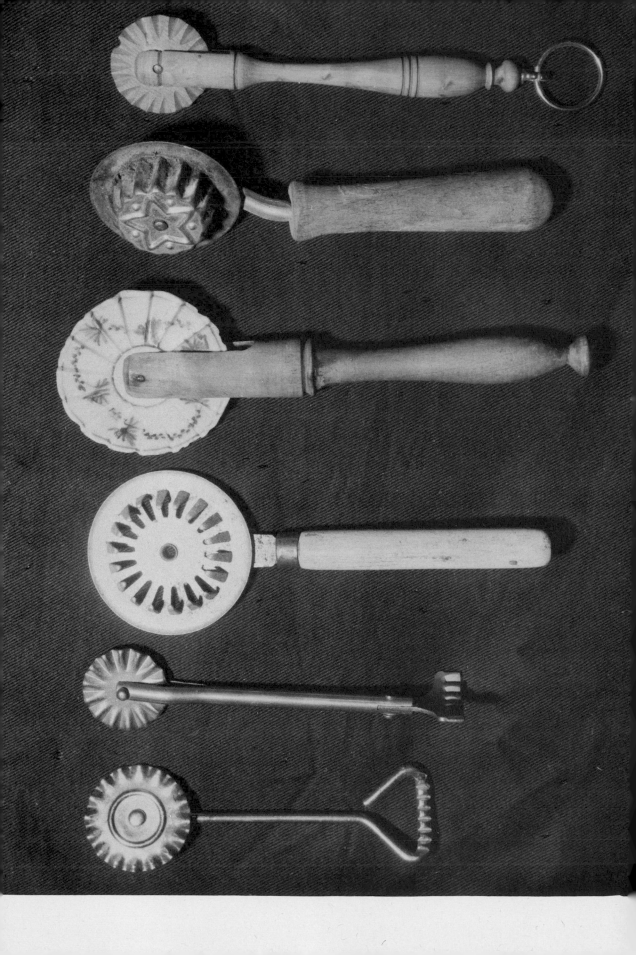

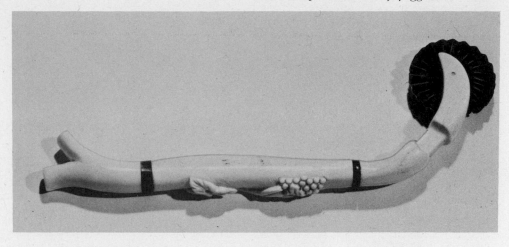

A pie lifter was used to remove hot pies from the brick bake oven and, later, from the range oven. Two-pronged, spring-tined pie lifters called "pie forks" were twisted from heavy wire. Some of these had wooden handles; in others the wire was twisted to form a handle. Round, tin shovel-shaped pie lifters were used to transfer pies and other hot dishes from oven to table. Simple round wooden paddles with short or long arms were easily made hot pie and bread lifters. In the 1910s, a wire hot-pan lifter worked by a thumb lever on the wooden handle; it sold for 25¢.

Carved whalebone pie crimper. *Courtesy Mystic Seaport; photo by Louis S. Martel*

Pie crimpers and pastry jaggers. *Top to bottom:* Machine-made wood, twentieth-century; tinplated head, marked "DANDY PAT. APR. 28, 1925"; Meissen china head, nineteenth-century; aluminum head, marked "Vaughan's Pie Trimmer & Sealer PAT'D 5-10-21"; cast brass, nineteenth-century; nickel-plated, twentieth-century

Pots and Pans

Pots and pans have long been the mainstay of the kitchen. The earliest earthen vessels and cast-iron pots often held the whole meal in their vast innards. Old cast-iron pots weighed up to 120 pounds and held as much as forty gallons—truly back-breakers. Such huge pots were needed not only for cooking, but for candle-dipping, yarn-dyeing, soap-making, and clothes-boiling.

The three-legged, long-handled spider with low sides and the sturdy, covered Dutch oven with coals on its lid stood right in the fireplace among the hot coals. It is said that food baked in a Dutch oven was beyond compare. Various-sized kettles and cauldrons hung from the lug-pole or crane, or were suspended from trammels and pot hooks. The three-legged gypsy kettle, holding a gallon or more, either hung from its bail handle or was placed in the glowing embers.

Copper pots were quicker to heat and lighter, but more expensive, and few families were fortunate enough to possess them. An unusual eighteenth-century piece is a pan made of wrought sheet-copper with high iron legs and a long handle decoratively riveted on.

Cast-iron frying pans, pots, kettles, and tea-kettles were the usual cooking implements of the nineteenth century; and the coal or wood stove replaced the fireplace during this century as the source of heat for cooking. Many of these cooking

From Van Heusen-Charles Co. Catalog, 1898

**ROYAL SELF-BASTING ROASTER
AND BAKING PANS.**

vessels had recessed bottoms made to fit into the lid openings of the stoves. An elaborate iron cooker with its own fuel container in the bottom was called the "Yankee Baker, Yankee Cook." It was made about 1869 by Orbeton and Lang of Haverhill, Massachusetts.

Copper six-quart jelly kettles and double boilers

From Ladies' Home Journal, Nov. 1921

were prized possessions. Copper saucepans and saucepots from one quart to eight quarts capacity had matching lids and brass handles with hanging holes. The teakettles had lapped seams or dovetailed seams and wooden or milk-glass handles on the bails. Pre-1880 water kettles of brass had dovetailed joints, swan spouts, and iron handles. Milk pans of brass, 16 inches in diameter, were dairy-room adjuncts. Brass and copper cooking utensils were difficult to keep bright. They were usually tin-lined for ease of cleaning and to prevent corrosion. Worn tin linings should be renewed as the chemical reaction of certain food acids with copper or brass may make one ill.

From Boston Directory, 1869

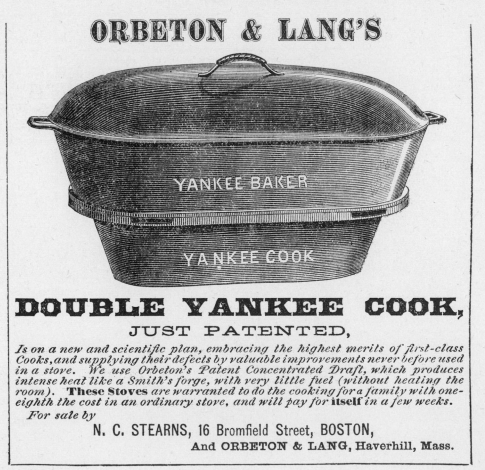

ORBETON & LANG'S

YANKEE BAKER

YANKEE COOK

DOUBLE YANKEE COOK,

JUST PATENTED,

Is on a new and scientific plan, embracing the highest merits of first-class Cooks, and supplying their defects by valuable improvements never before used in a stove. We use Orbeton's Patent Concentrated Draft, which produces intense heat like a Smith's forge, with very little fuel (without heating the room). **These Stoves** *are warranted to do the cooking for a family with one-eighth the cost in an ordinary stove, and will pay for* **itself** *in a few weeks.*

For sale by

N. C. STEARNS, 16 Bromfield Street, BOSTON,

And ORBETON & LANG, Haverhill, Mass.

OVAL HAM BOILER.
Tinned and Porcelain Lined.
75 to $1.50.

Pots and pans of all descriptions were made of tin in the nineteenth century. There were dairy pans, round and oval pudding pans, bread pans, shallow and deep stew pans, oyster-stew pans, milk or rice boilers, and fry pans. The asparagus boilers and fish kettles each had lift-out trivets. Some of these articles had copper bottoms for more even heating, and the bottoms could be replaced when worn.

Graniteware pots and pans came in the same shapes as the tin ones. Most could be purchased with either tin or graniteware lids. Graniteware was advertised widely and used extensively in the late nineteenth and early twentieth centuries.

From Van Heusen-Charles Co. Catalog, 1898

From Biddle Hardware Co. Catalog, 1910

"OVAL OAK" SEAMLESS ROASTER

Vapors Condense on Low Points of the Oak Tree Top and Drip Evenly over the Roast.

No. 87 "Oval Oak," 10⅝ x 16¾ x 7½ inches --Per dozen $11.50
Half dozen in a Case.

FARINA BOILERS.

Quarts,		3	4	
Per Doz		.5.00	6.50	8

FARINA SAUCEPANS.

Quarts,		3	4	
Per Doz		.5.25	6.75	8

MILK BOILERS.

Quarts,		2	4	
Per Doz		10.50	16.50	20

SAUCEPANS.

Quarts,	2	3	4
Per Doz	2.50	3.00	4.00

COPPER BOTTOM SAUCEPANS

Quarts,	2	3	4
Per Doz	3.75	4.00	5.00

From U.S. Stamping Co. Catalog, Jan. 1883

Lightweight, durable aluminum almost monopolized the cookware market in the early 1900s. It largely replaced the cumbersome iron utensils, the eternally chipping graniteware, and the expensive difficult-to-clean brass and copper pots and pans. However, the cast-iron frying pan still held its stalwart post, and many modern gourmet cooks still favor it.

ASPARAGUS BOILERS—XX.

Inches,	12x7x6¾
Per Doz.	15.50

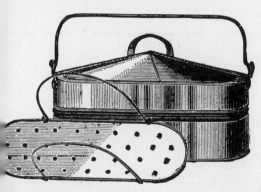

FISH KETTLES—IXXX.

Inches,	18	20	22	24
Each	2.67	3.00	3.25	3.85

*From U.S. Stamping Co.
Catalog, Jan. 1883*

"POTMEND"

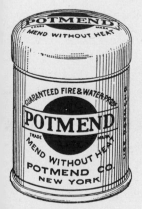

Water, Fire and Acid Proof. Repair without Heat (Mix only with a few drops of Cold Water) any article made of Agate, China, Enamel, Porcelain, Aluminum, Glass, Wood, Marble, Meerschaum, Amber, Ivory, Bronze, Tin, Leather, Copper, Rubber, Iron, etc.

"Potmend"___Per dozen $1.80

One dozen in a Box.

*From Biddle Hardware
Co. Catalog, 1910*

Rolling Pins

Rolling pins were used for flattening out pie-crust dough, cookies, wafers, biscuits, and crackers. Wooden rolling pins are the oldest and were the most common, some being nothing more than cylinders of wood. The woods most frequently used in early America were maple, beech, applewood, lignum vitae, cherry, walnut, pine, and sycamore. Knob-ended rolling pins preceded those with the handles carved in one piece with the roller. Tapered rolling pins with thick centers which diminished gradually to narrow ends were called French rolling pins. These may still be purchased today in kitchen specialty shops. The rolling pins with handles which remained stationary as the barrel rotated have remained popular for years.

Inlays of darker woods, such as cherry, mahogany, and walnut, added interest to some of the wooden rolling pins. These embellishments were usually in the shapes of hearts, circles, and diamonds. Sailors at sea carved distinctive rolling pins of lignum vitae with inlaid pegs of whalebone. These were often made as companion pieces to the scrimshawed whalebone pie crimpers. The less artistic seamen simply added ivory handles to pins of lignum vitae.

Rolling pins. *Top to bottom:* French-style with tapering ends; maple with mahogany handles; one-piece birch wood

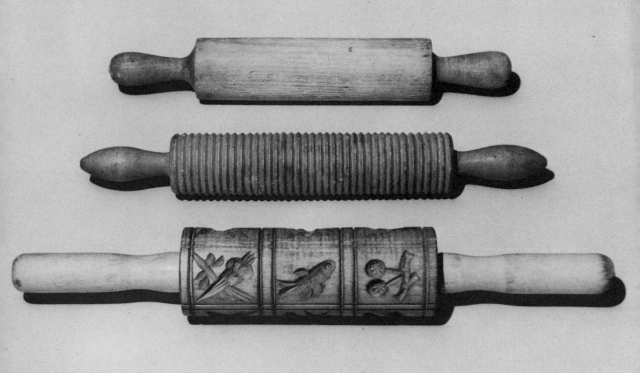

Wooden rolling pins with grooves cut into their barrels were used for making cookies. These rollers gave the cookies a corrugated surface and were also used for rolling out hardtack, a coarse, unsalted cracker. Old hand-carved rolling pins were produced in Germany for the making of springerle, a type of delicious, traditional Christmas cookie. The designs on these pins were the quaint figures of animals, fruits, and flowers, each carved in a square outline. Such rolling pins are still being made in Germany today. Flat springerle boards carved with the same designs were pressed into the rolled-out cookie dough to transfer their designs.

Hollow, bottle-type, glass rolling pins with screw caps or cork closures originally came filled with baking powder, vinegar, cocoa, or bath salts. Filled with cracked ice or ice water, these pins chilled the dough and kept it at a good working temperature. Clear-glass and milk-glass rolling

Top to bottom: Small, only 11½ in. long, one-piece rolling pin; corrugated cookie roller; springerle roller

Clear-glass bottle rolling
pin with screw-on cap

GLASS ROLLING PINS.

*From Van Heusen-
Charles Co. Catalog, 1898*

Meissen onion pattern
rolling pin, nineteenth-
century

pins with stationary wooden handles could be
chilled in the icebox. Elaborate, hollow, blown-
glass rolling pins in clear, emerald green, cobalt
blue, and milk glass bore enameled decorations
and inscriptions. Their nautical embellishments
and mottoes hint that they were probably gifts
from sailors. Most of these were English. Some
were made of Nailsea-type flecked or swirled glass
in a variety of colors.

Pottery and china rolling pins were popular in
the nineteenth century. Delft-type windmill and
sailboat designs were prevalent. The blue-and-
white Meissen onion pattern porcelain rolling
pins may date from the seventeenth century. This
pattern is being copied today in a crude imitation
of Meissen. These cheap copies bear an easily
removed "Japan" paper label. Complete canister
sets for sugar, flour, and spices were made to
match most of these patterns. Pie crimpers,
twirlers, meat tenderizers, and other utensils could
be purchased to match the centuries-old Meissen
pattern. Twirlers had wooden or pottery star-
shaped heads attached to a wooden handle about
nine to twelve inches long. The head was placed
in the bottom of the bowl of ingredients; the

handle was pressed tightly between the palms and as the hands were moved rapidly back and forth the tool rotated or "twirled" and thus mixed the ingredients. The Delft and Meissen kitchen utensils are attractive examples of combined utility and beauty.

Yellow pottery mixing bowls were useful and durable. Large rolling pins of this heavy, coarse, yellow pottery were sturdy-appearing tools.

Tin rolling pins usually had a companion tin pastry sheet. Tin, too, took well to chilling. Since the dough was less likely to stick to a tin pastry sheet and roller, flour was not needed to dust the work board. This was a practical and different pastry set, probably patented.

Cast-iron rolling pins have been seen, but it is likely that they were for some other purpose than cooking.

A pastry blender was an instrument used to mix and blend pastry dough. It usually consisted of about seven springy steel wires bent into the form of a U with the ends of the wires retained in a sturdy metal end piece bolted to a wooden or

Two springy wire pastry blenders, both made by Androck and patented in 1929; the one on the left has a Bakelite handle, the other handle is wooden

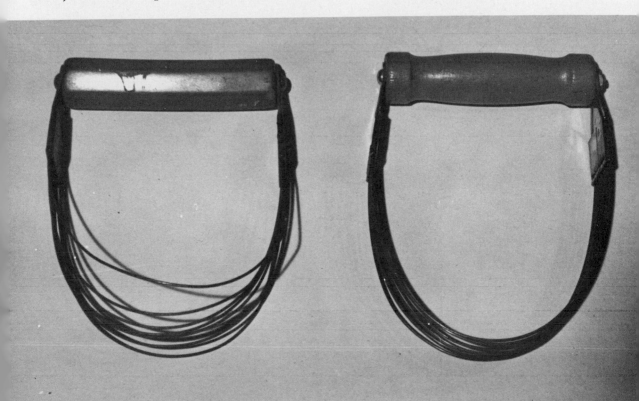

Bakelite handle. The most common blender of this type was one marked "Androck," patented November 12, 1929. Stirring pastry tends to toughen it by developing the gluten of the flour; the cutting-in motion of a pastry blender tends to produce a light and tender pastry.

"Bakelite" is a trade name for a synthetic resin with properties similar to modern plastic. Prior to 1925 this hard, rigid, strong material was used little on housewares. Early molded Bakelite parts were used mainly in radio sets, electrical outlets, and automobiles. In the mid-twenties, because it is a poor conductor of heat and stays cool to the touch, it began to be used for handles for teapots, coffeepots, irons, and other housewares.

The simplest and probably the oldest scale was the "even balance" scale, with a center fulcrum and two arms of the same length. Old ones made of wrought iron hung from a center hook. Later cast-iron ones were held by a post in the middle. A pan or scoop hung from one side held the article to be weighed; a pan suspended from the other side held the weights. Butter scales were balance scales made all of wood or of iron with flat porcelain platforms.

Steelyard scales have been in use since the days of the ancient Romans. Small ones were called a "steel foot." A sliding weight balanced the scales in an off-center manner. Some had a brass beam and weight.

Grocer and market scales in the 1800s were of several varieties. There were dial scales, beam scales, platform scales, and spring scales. Huge portable platform scales rolled on wheels and weighed goods from 500 to 1,500 pounds. The beams on these were highly polished brass; the pillar and cap were of hardwood. Counter-top scoop scales with brass or tin scoops had a round dial, a brass beam with hanging weights, or a balance platform for iron weights. Some of the dial scales had the weighing platform on top of the scale; others had the scale side by side with the scoop holder.

Hanging spring scales usually had brass fronts. Some were cylindrical; others were flat. The cylindrical ones were called sportsman's scales and usually had a capacity of 15 pounds. The pointer, operated by a coiled wire, indicated the weight of the object suspended from the lower hook. The vanishing "rag-bone men" customarily used flat spring scales, most of which had a maximum capacity of from 25 to 150 pounds.

Scales

Butchers and grocers sometimes used spring scales with circular dials. The produce or meat was placed in a scoop or on a round iron pan hung from the bottom hook. The pans were usually enameled; the scoops were tin or galvanized. Spring scales were, generally, not as accurate as the beam balance type.

Facing page: Wrought-iron steelyard, circa 1750. *Courtesy Colonial Williamsburg*

Hanging, left: Iron steelyard scale; *right:* Brass-faced spring scales and a white-enameled round-faced spring scale. *Bottom:* Balance scales with weights and a Columbian Postal Scale patented 1896

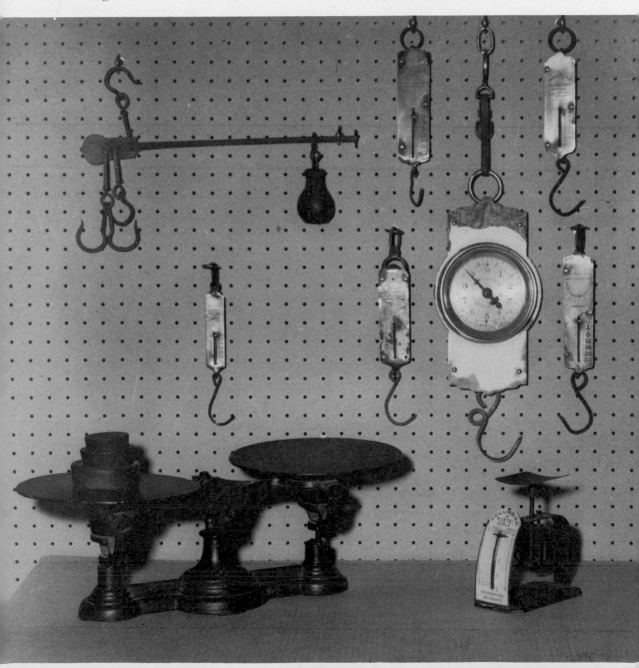

CHATILLON'S
SPRING BALANCES

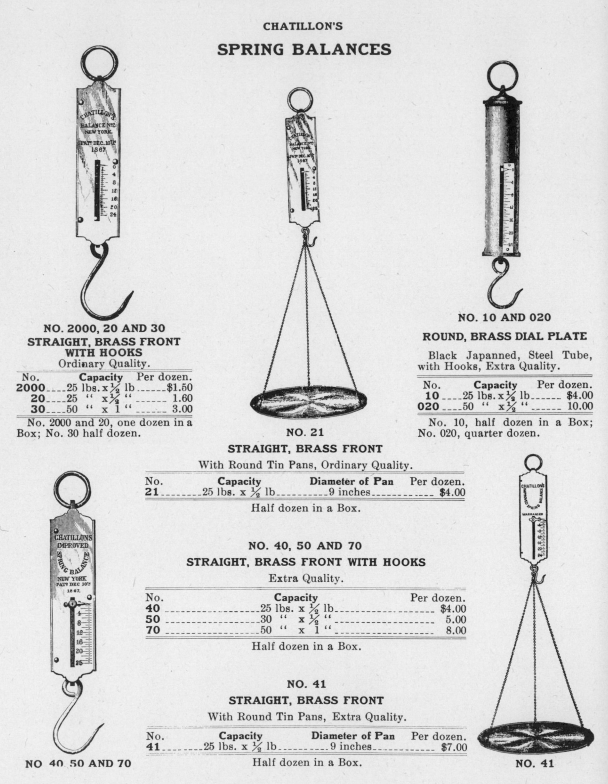

NO. 2000, 20 AND 30
STRAIGHT, BRASS FRONT WITH HOOKS
Ordinary Quality.

No.	Capacity	Per dozen.
2000	25 lbs. x ½ lb	$1.50
20	25 " x ½ "	1.60
30	50 " x 1 "	3.00

No. 2000 and 20, one dozen in a Box; No. 30 half dozen.

NO. 10 AND 020
ROUND, BRASS DIAL PLATE

Black Japanned, Steel Tube, with Hooks, Extra Quality.

No.	Capacity	Per dozen.
10	25 lbs. x ½ lb	$4.00
020	50 " x ½ "	10.00

No. 10, half dozen in a Box; No. 020, quarter dozen.

NO. 21
STRAIGHT, BRASS FRONT
With Round Tin Pans, Ordinary Quality.

No.	Capacity	Diameter of Pan	Per dozen.
21	25 lbs. x ½ lb	9 inches	$4.00

Half dozen in a Box.

NO. 40, 50 AND 70
STRAIGHT, BRASS FRONT WITH HOOKS
Extra Quality.

No.	Capacity	Per dozen.
40	25 lbs. x ½ lb	$4.00
50	30 " x ½ "	5.00
70	50 " x 1 "	8.00

Half dozen in a Box.

NO. 41
STRAIGHT, BRASS FRONT
With Round Tin Pans, Extra Quality.

No.	Capacity	Diameter of Pan	Per dozen.
41	25 lbs. x ½ lb	9 inches	$7.00

Half dozen in a Box.

NO 40 50 AND 70

NO. 41

From Biddle Hardware Co. Catalog, 1910

CHATILLON'S
SPRING BALANCES

NO. 80 TO 100A

STRAIGHT, BRASS FRONT, WITH HOOKS

Extra Quality.

No.	Capacity	Per dozen.
80	80 lbs. x 1 lb	$24.00
90	100 " x 1 "	42.00
100	125 " x 1 "	48.00
100A	150 " x 1 "	60.00

No. 80, quarter dozen in a Box, other numbers, one-twelfth dozen.

NO. 150

"IRON CLAD" ICE BALANCES, WITH HOOK

Malleable Iron Cases, Black Japanned and Ornamented, Nickel Plated Brass Dial Plates.

No.	Capacity	Per dozen.
150	200 lbs x 5 lbs	$54.00

One twelfth dozen in a Box.

NO. 80 TO 100A

NO. 150, ICE

NO. 231 AND 241

CIRCULAR, BRASS FRONT

With Round Tin Pans.

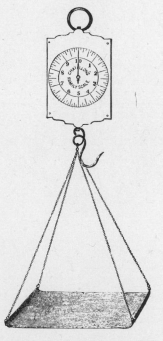

No.	Capacity	Diameter of Pans	Each.
231	10 lbs. x ½ oz	11 inches	$3.50
241	20 " x 1 "	11 "	3.75

Three in a Box.

NO. 232, 242 AND 252

CIRCULAR, BRASS FRONT

With Square Tin Pans.

No.	Capacity	Size of Pans	Each.
232	10 lbs. x ½ oz	10½ x 12 inches	$3.75
242	20 " x 1 "	10½ x 12 "	4.00
252	15 " x ½ "	10½ x 12 "	6.25

No. 232 and No. 242, three in a Box; No. 252, one in a Box.

No. 252 weighs the Full Capacity with three Revolutions of Pointer. Each 5 lbs. marked on the Slide and Intermediate Weights on the Circle.

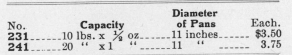

NO. 231 AND 241

NO. 232 AND 242, STYLE OF NO. 252

From Biddle Hardware Co. Catalog, 1910

CHATILLON'S

SPRING BALANCES

NO. 144E, CIRCULAR

6 inch Silver Plated Brass Dial, with White Enameled Pan and Tinned Iron Bows.

No.	Capacity	Diameter of Pan	Each.
144E	24 lbs. x 1 oz	11 inches	$4.65

One in a Box.

NO. 250, CIRCULAR

Brass Front, with Hook. Each 5 lbs. marked on the Slide and Intermediate Weights on the Circle. Weighs Full Capacity with three Revolutions of Pointer.

No.	Capacity	Each.
250	15 lbs. x ½ oz	$5.50

One in a Box.

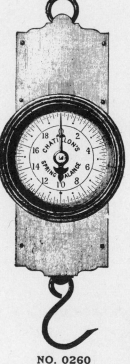

NO. 144E

NO. 250

NO. 0260, CIRCULAR

5 inch Dial, with White Enameled Front and Glass Sash. Each 10 lbs. marked on the Slide and Intermediate Weights on the Dial. Weighs Full Capacity with three Revolutions of Pointer.

No.	Capacity	Each.
0260	30 lbs. x 1 oz	$6.50

One in a Box.

NO. 261, CIRCULAR

Brass Front. Round Tin Pans.

No.	Capacity	Diameter of Pan	Each.
261	30 lbs. x 1 oz	11 inches	$5.75
271	60 " x 2 "	13 "	7.00

One in a Box.

No. 261, each, 10 lbs; No. 271, each, 20 lbs. marked on the Slide and Intermediate Weights on the Circle. Weighs Full Capacity with three Revolutions of the Pointer.

NO. 0260

NO. 261 AND 271

From Biddle Hardware Co. Catalog, 1910

CHATILLON'S
SPRING BALANCES

NO. 0261, CIRCULAR

5 inch Dial with White Enameled Front and Glass Sash, Round Tin Pans, each 10 lbs. marked on the Slide and Intermediate Weights on the Dial.

No.	Capacity	Diameter of Pan	Each.
0261	30 lbs. x 1 oz	11 inches	$6.75

One in a Box.

NO. 0261

NO. 262 AND 272, CIRCULAR

Brass Front, Square Tin Pans.

No.	Capacity	Size of Pans	Each.
262	30 lbs. x 1 oz	10½x12 in	$6.25
272	60 " x 2 "	11½x12 "	7.50

One in a Box.

No. 262, each 10 lbs.; No. 272, each 20 lbs. marked on the Slide and Intermediate Weights on the Circle.

All the above weigh Full Capacity with three Revolutions of Pointer.

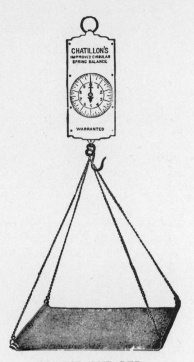

NO. 262 AND 272

NO. 0262 AND 0272, CIRCULAR

5 inch Dial with White Enameled Front and Glass Sash, Square Tin Pans.

No.	Capacity	Size of Pans	Each.
0262	30 lbs. x 1 oz	10½x12 in	$7.25
0272	60 " x 2 "	11½x12 "	8.50

One in a Box.

No. 0262, each 10 lbs.; No. 0272, each 20 lbs. marked on the Slide and Intermediate Weights on the Dial.

NO. 264 AND 275, CIRCULAR
BRASS FRONT

With Tinned Pan, Tinned Iron Bows and Swivels.

No.	Capacity	Diameter of Pan	Each.
264	30 lbs. x 1 oz	13 inches	$7.25

With Tin Pan, Brass Bows and Swivels.

No.	Capacity	Diameter of Pan	Each.
275	60 lbs. x 2 oz	13 inches	$9.50

One in a Box.

No. 264, each 10 lbs.; No. 275, each 20 lbs. marked on the Slide, and Intermediate Weights on the Circle.

All the above weigh Full Capacity with three Revolutions of Pointer.

NO. 0262 AND 0272

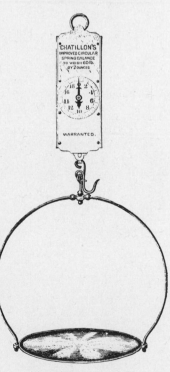

NO. 264 AND 275

From Biddle Hardware Co. Catalog, 1910

NO. 0264 TO 0266

NO. 5266 E

CHATILLON'S
SPRING BALANCES
NO. 0264 TO 0266, CIRCULAR

5 inch Dial with White Enameled Front and Glass Sash.
With Tin Pans, Tinned Iron Bows and Swivels.

No.	Capacity	Diameter of Pan	Each.
0264	30 lbs. x 1 oz.	13 in.	$8.25
0274	60 " x 2 "	13 "	9.75

With Tin Pans, Brass Bows and Swivels.

0265	30 lbs. x 1 oz.	13 in.	$9.00
0275	60 " x 2 "	13 "	10.50

With Brass Pans, Brass Bows and Swivels.

0266	30 lbs. x 1 oz.	13 in.	$11.00

One in a Box.
No. 0264, 0265 and 0266, each 10 lbs., and No. 0274 and 0275, each 20 lbs., marked on the Slide, and Intermediate Weights on the Dial.

NO. 5266 EH, CIRCULAR
7 inch Dial with White Enameled Front and Glass Sash, 13 inch White Enameled Pans without Rims, Tinned Iron Bows and Swivels.

No.	Each.
5266EH	30 lbs. x 1 oz. $12.00

One in a Box.
Each 10 lbs. marked on the Slide and Intermediate Weights on the Dial.

NO. 5266 E CIRCULAR

7 inch Dial with White Enameled Front and Glass Sash, Porcelain Enameled Pans, 13 inches diameter, with German Silver Rims and Nickel Plated Bows.

No.	Each.
5266E	30 lbs. x 1 oz. $9.00

One in a Box.
Each 10 lbs. marked on the Slide and Intermediate Weights on the Dial.

NO. 4266 E, CIRCULAR

Large 8 inch Dial and 10 inch Glass Sash, Porcelain Enameled Pans, 13 inches diameter with German Silver Rims and Nickel Plated Bows.

No.	Each.
4266E	30 lbs. x 1 oz. $10.00

One in a Box.
Each 10 lbs. marked on the Slide and Intermediate Weights on the Dial.

All the above Weigh Full Capacity with Three Revolutions of Pointer.

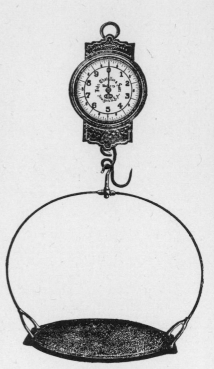

NO. 5266 EH

NO. 4266E

From Biddle Hardware Co. Catalog, 1910

COMPARATIVE LIST OF SPRING BALANCES

Chatillon	No.	2000	20	30	21	10	020	40	50	70	41	80	90	100	100A	150
Landers, Frary & Clark	"	3	50	51	52	70	273	81	82	84	91	86	87	88	88A	302

Chatillon	No.	231	241	232	242	252	144E	250	0260	261	271	0261	262	272
Landers, Frary & Clark	"	76	77	76½	77½	119S	475E	119	0120W	123	124	01123	126	127

Chatillon	No.	0262	0272	264	275	0264	0274	0265	0275	0266	5266EH	5266E	4266E
Landers, Frary & Clark	"	0126	0127	150	141	0150	0151	0140	0141	0143	430	0030E7	0030E

COLUMBIA FAMILY SCALES

NO. 502 AND 1502

NO. 102, 104½ AND 1100

SHEET STEEL, BLACK ENAMEL FINISH, DECORATED IN GILT
Regulated by Brass Screw on Top.

No.												Each.
502	Slanting Dial, Weighs 24 pounds x 1 ounce, White Enameled Dial, Square Steel Top, without Scoop											$1.20
1502	" " " 24 " x 1 " " " " " " " with Tin											1.40
102	Straight " " 24 " x 1 " " " " " " " without											1.30
104½	" " " 24 " x 1 " " " " White Enam. " " "											1.50
1100	" " " 24 " x 1 " " " " Round Steel " with Tin "											1.50

One in a Box. Six in a Case.

NO. 162 AND 1162

SHEET STEEL, BLACK ENAMEL FINISH

Decorated in Gilt.

Regulated by Brass Screw on Top.

Large 8 inch Dial, with Clear Plain Figures.

Square Steel Top.

No.		Each.
162	Weighs 60 pounds x 2 ounces, without Scoop	$2.75
1162	" 60 " x 2 " with Tin "	3.25

One in a Box. Six in a Case.

NO. 162 AND 1162

From Biddle Hardware Co. Catalog, 1910

TEA AND COUNTER SCALES

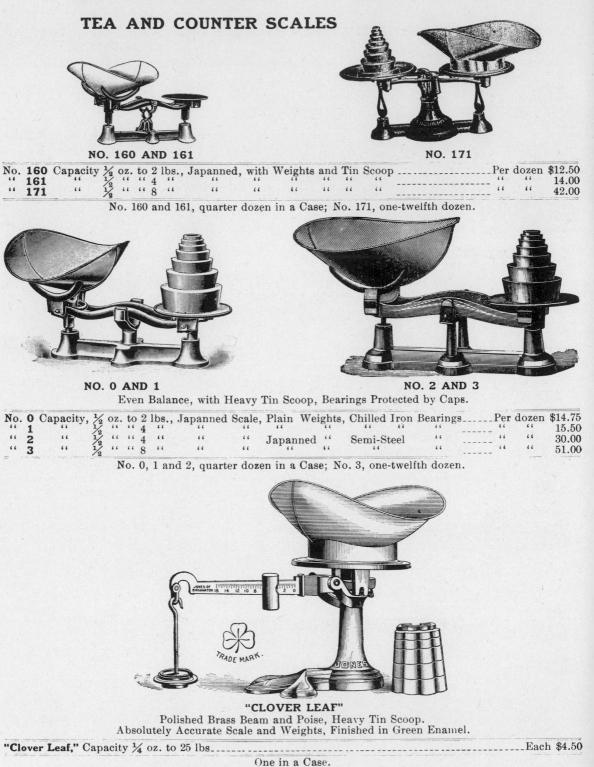

NO. 160 AND 161

NO. 171

No. **160**	Capacity	½ oz. to 2 lbs.,	Japanned, with Weights and Tin Scoop								Per dozen	$12.50
" **161**	"	½ " " 4 "	"	"	"	"	"	"	"	"	"	"	14.00
" **171**	"	½ " " 8 "	"	"	"	"	"	"	"		"	"	42.00

No. 160 and 161, quarter dozen in a Case; No. 171, one-twelfth dozen.

NO. 0 AND 1

NO. 2 AND 3

Even Balance, with Heavy Tin Scoop, Bearings Protected by Caps.

No. **0**	Capacity,	½ oz. to 2 lbs.,	Japanned Scale, Plain Weights, Chilled Iron Bearings								Per dozen	$14.75
" **1**	"	½ " " 4 "	"	"	"	"	"	"	"		"	"	15.50
" **2**	"	½ " " 4 "	"	"		Japanned "	Semi-Steel	"		"	"	30.00
" **3**	"	½ " " 8 "	"	"		"	"	"		"	"	51.00

No. 0, 1 and 2, quarter dozen in a Case; No. 3, one-twelfth dozen.

"CLOVER LEAF"

Polished Brass Beam and Poise, Heavy Tin Scoop.
Absolutely Accurate Scale and Weights, Finished in Green Enamel.

"Clover Leaf," Capacity ¼ oz. to 25 lbs.		Each $4.50

One in a Case.

From Biddle Hardware Co. Catalog, 1910

PLATFORM SCALES

PORTABLE, ON WHEELS

Hardwood Pillars, Caps and Platform Boards, finished in Natural Color. Polished Brass Beam and Sliding Poise. Tool Steel Pivots. Iron Parts, Japanned. Each Scale carefully Sealed to U. S. Standard Weights. Capacity, 600 lbs. Beam, 50 lbs. x ¼ lb. Platform, 16 x 25 inches.

Each _____ $16.00

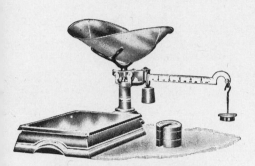

UNION PLATFORM SCALES

No. **3, Empire,** Japanned, Nickel Plated Steel Beam, Hanging Poise, Tin Scoop. Capacity, 240 lbs. x ½ oz _____ Each $5.00

One in a Case.

SCALE WEIGHTS

ADJUSTED

Weights	Not Japanned, per dozen.	German Bronzed, per dozen.	Cast Brass, each.	Quantity in a Box
½ Ounce	.23	.27	.25	3 Dozen
1 "	.32	.36	.59	3 "
2 "	.45	.54	.81	3 "
4 "	.63	.77	1.04	2 "
8 "	1.08	1.35	1.35	2 "
1 Pound	1.62	2.16	1.62	In Bulk
2 "	2.70	3.51	3.24	" "
4 "	5.13	6.75	5.67	" "
8 "	9.72	13.50	9.72	" "

Weights in Sets	Not Japanned, per set.	German Bronzed, per set.	Cast Brass, per set.	Quantity in Package
½ oz. to 1 lb.	.32	.36	2.93	1 Set
½ " " 2 "	.54	.68	5.40	1 "
½ " " 4 "	.99	1.17	9.90	1 "
½ " " 8 "	1.80	2.16	18.00	1 "

P. S. & W.
SCALE BEAMS AND POISES

JAPANNED, WITH WHITE FIGURES AND GOLD STRIPES

To Weigh, pounds	100	150	200	250	300	360	400	450	500	600	700	800
"King Cotton" Each	$1.50	1.50	1.60	1.90	2.10	2.50	2.90	3.20	3.50	4.00	4.66	5.30

500 Pounds and under, half dozen in a Case, with Poises; 600 to 800 Pounds, Poises separate.

POISES, SEPARATE

Pounds	1	2	3	4	5	6	8	12	16	20	24	32
Each	.25	.30	.40	.50	.60	.70	.85	1.10	1.50	1.70	2.40	2.90

From Biddle Hardware Co. Catalog, 1910

CHATILLON'S
SCALE BEAMS AND POISES

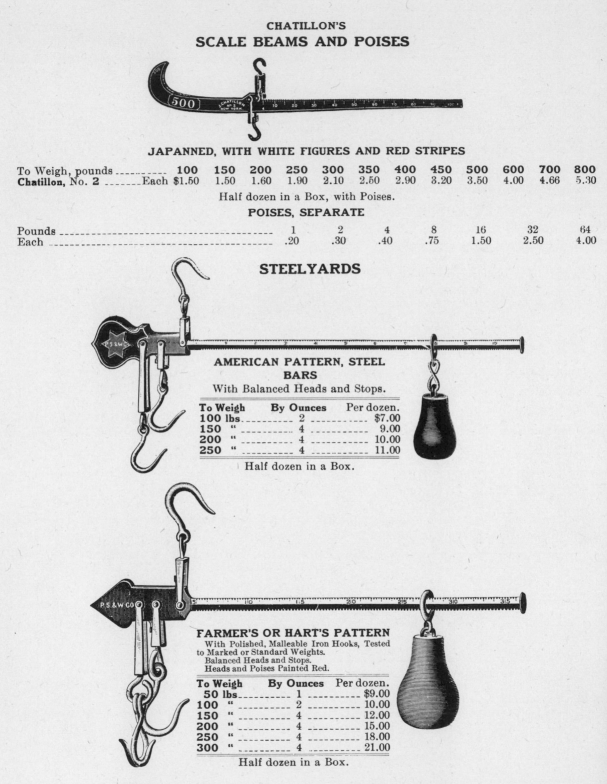

JAPANNED, WITH WHITE FIGURES AND RED STRIPES

To Weigh, pounds	100	150	200	250	300	350	400	450	500	600	700	800
Chatillon, No. 2 ____Each	$1.50	1.50	1.60	1.90	2.10	2.50	2.90	3.20	3.50	4.00	4.66	5.30

Half dozen in a Box, with Poises.

POISES, SEPARATE

Pounds	1	2	4	8	16	32	64
Each	.20	.30	.40	.75	1.50	2.50	4.00

STEELYARDS

AMERICAN PATTERN, STEEL BARS
With Balanced Heads and Stops.

To Weigh	By Ounces	Per dozen.
100 lbs.	2	$7.00
150 "	4	9.00
200 "	4	10.00
250 "	4	11.00

Half dozen in a Box.

FARMER'S OR HART'S PATTERN
With Polished, Malleable Iron Hooks, Tested to Marked or Standard Weights. Balanced Heads and Stops. Heads and Poises Painted Red.

To Weigh	By Ounces	Per dozen.
50 lbs	1	$9.00
100 "	2	10.00
150 "	4	12.00
200 "	4	15.00
250 "	4	18.00
300 "	4	21.00

Half dozen in a Box.

From Biddle Hardware Co. Catalog, 1910

Eighteenth-century flour, meal, and sugar sifters were round or oval wooden hoop frames fitted with horsehair or thin wire mesh sifters. Strainers were pierced tin box- or cup-shaped utensils, and were often combination strainers and graters. The rough side of the hand-pierced tin strainers was used for grating and the reverse, smoother side for straining. Small tea strainers were woven entirely of brass wire. Large bowllike sieves were called cullenders or, later, colanders. These were made of pierced tin, copper, or brass, and usually had handles and a rim base. Pierced-tin scoop-shaped sieves sifted sand to scour the iron cooking vessels. Some sieves were made of perforated leather, but these were not durable as they dried and split from usage.

Grains were winnowed in large, heavy sieves made from splints. Winnowing sieves or baskets were used years ago by the Indians to separate the chaff from the grain of the wild rice which grew in the Great Lakes region.

Sieves were also made from an oblong piece of solid wood. A bowl like depression was carved in the center and pierced with holes. Long "arms" left on each side supported the sieve on the bowl or pot.

Two of the first patented tin sifters were similar in appearance, and both were combination scoops and sifters. One was Earnshaw's patent of 1866; the other was the Bucknam Improved Combination Sifter, patented the same year. The Hunter Sifter, patented 1879, and the National Flour Sifter more nearly resembled our modern ones. The widely imitated Hunter could also be used as a scoop, a measure, or a strainer. A toy sifter, an exact replica of the full-sized Hunter sifter, was offered in magazine ads in 1890 for three

Sifters, Strainers, and Funnels

The Hunter Sifter combines twelve kitchen utensils in one. It is a Mixer, Scoop, Measure, Weigher, Dredger, Rice Washer, and Tomato, Pumpkin, Starch, Wine and Fruit Strainer. It is the most useful kitchen utensil made.

For sale at stove, hardware, and house-furnishing stores.

A toy Sifter, the size of the above cut, which shows how the large Sifter works, and which will afford amusement to any little girl, will be sent free to any one who will mention where this advertisement was seen, and enclose three two-cent stamps for postage to

THE FRED. J. MEYERS MFG. CO.
COVINGTON, KY.

215

"Acme" sifter, patented
1902

"Duplex" sifter, patented
1922

Extension sifter

two-cent stamps. The Magic Flour Sifter was a sort of fine wire basket with a tin handle to hold and shake it by. The Standard Sifter and Fruit Strainer, patented March 12, 1878, was manufactured by The Washington Stamping Company. The Acme Sifter was patented November 4, 1902, and the five-cup Duplex Sifter manufactured by the Uneek Utilities Corporation, Chicago, was patented in 1922.

A versatile extension strainer, circa 1890, was a large strainer set in an oblong wire frame which could be adjusted to fit different-sized bowls. Simple tin-sided tea strainers with wooden handles were often "give-aways" with advertisements imprinted on their handles or embossed on the tin sides. One advertised the old C. D. Kenny Company, a well-known Eastern wholesale grocer. Gravy strainers were bowl-shaped tin strainers with a single handle. Jelly strainers were similar in shape, as were the larger soup strainers. Milk strainers were tin strainers of large diameter with collar bases and wire bottoms. In the days when flour, sugar, meal, salt, and spices required sifting,

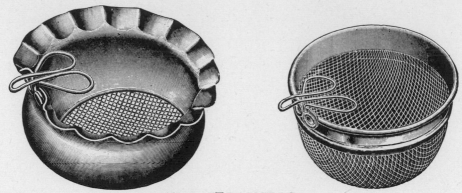

TEA STRAINERS.

Will not drip. Attached to mouth of Teapot.

5 and 10 cts.

From Van Heusen-Charles Co. Catalog, 1898

COAL SIEVES

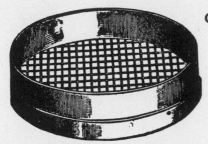

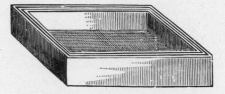

WOOD RIM, ROUND

Diameter	Ash Rim	Oak Rim
All 12 inches_____Per dozen $1.80		2.80
" 14 " _____ " " 2.20		3.20
12 and 14 in., assorted " " 2.00		3.00
With Handles. add_____ " " .80		.80

One dozen in a Bundle.

WOOD RIM, SQUARE, PAINTED

3 in a Nest $\begin{cases} 10 \times 12 \\ 12 \times 14 \\ 14 \times 16 \end{cases}$ inches_____ Per dozen $2.50

2 in a Nest $\begin{cases} 12 \times 14 \\ 14 \times 16 \end{cases}$ inches_____ " " 3.00

With Handles, add _____ " " .80

One dozen Nests in a Bundle.

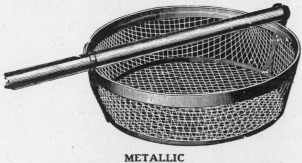

METALLIC

Frame of Sheet Metal and Sieve of Wire Cloth, Stained Handles.

Metallic, All Japanned, with Handles_Per dozen $4.00
Extra Handles_____ " " .80

Three dozen in a Crate.

CONVEX

Japanned Sheet Iron, Convex Bottom Stained Handles.

Convex, Japanned, with Handles___Per dozen $4.00
" Galvanized, " " ___ " " 5.50
Extra Handles_____ " " .80

Three dozen in a Crate.

From Biddle Hardware Co. Catalog, 1910

EARNSHAW'S FLOUR SCOOP AND SIFTER.

Per Doz..8.75

NATIONAL FLOUR SIFTER.

Per Gro...40.00
Per Doz... 3.50

MAGIC FLOUR SIFTERS.

Per Doz... 3.75

From U.S. Stamping Co. Catalog, Jan. 1883

TIN WARE

PIECED WARE

MILK STRAINER PAILS

No	306	308	310	312
Quarts	6	8	10	12
IC Per dozen	$4.20	5.00	5.60	6.30

MILK STRAINERS
With Brass Strainers.
Diameter, 9½ inches.

No. **10** Large____Per dozen $2.40

CORRUGATED FUNNELS

No	1	2	3
Quarts	¼	½	1
Plain Per dozen	.74	.90	1.20

From Biddle Hardware Co. Catalog, 1910

MRS. HUTCHINS'
STRAINER SPOONS

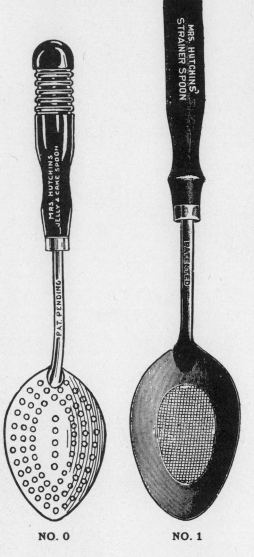

NO. 0   NO. 1

For Skimming Jelly or Soup or Poaching Eggs or Whipping Cream.

No. 0 Retinned, 12 inches long, Perforated,
        Black Enameled Handle ___Per dozen $1.50
  " 1 Retinned, 12 inches long, Gauze Wire
        Bottom, Plain Handle_____ Per dozen 1.50

sieving, and straining, these kitchen accessories were absolute necessities.

During the nineteenth century colanders were still being made in tin, copper, and brass, and were also being produced in the new graniteware.

Funnels were made in all sizes, from tiny to huge. They were made of wood, copper, tin, pressed and blown glass, pottery, china, pewter, and enamelware. Wooden ones were both hand-made and factory-made on the lathe. A white ironstone one was marked "SANITARY FRUIT JAR FUNNEL." Many were especially constructed for filling home-canning jars. A tin one, designed for canning jars, screwed to the jar top to prevent tipping; it was embossed "PAT. JUNE 29 97."

From Biddle Hardware Co. Catalog, 1910

Small tin funnel marked "C. D. Kenny Co.'s Teas—Coffees—Sugars"

Tin canning-jar funnel marked "patented June 29, 1897"

White pottery funnel marked "Sanitary Fruit Jar Funnel"

Soapstone

Soapstone is a bluish-gray, soft rock with a smooth, greasy feel like that of soap, from which characteristic its name is derived. It is native to America and is found in considerable variety along the Atlantic Coast and in California. The ease with which it may be worked, plus its power of resisting heat, led to its use for vessels for cooking, whence it was often called "potstone" in the seventeenth and eighteenth centuries. Old writers called it *lapis ollaris,* which likewise means "potstone." The ingenious Eskimos of northern Canada carved lamps out of soapstone in which to burn oil made from blubber. These primitive people were the original inventors of the blubber lamp. They also made simple stoves and kettles from the soapstone. Since soapstone will not corrode and is easily turned on the lathe and cut with knives or saws, it took naturally to being made into culinary vessels.

Soapstone was used in early America for sinks, stoves, water pipes, firebricks, footwarmers, inkwells, griddles, pots, pans, and other useful items. Sinks carved out of soapstone may be seen in Old Sturbridge Village in Sturbridge, Massachusetts. The Shelburne Museum in Shelburne, Vermont, has a stove with soapstone top and sides and an iron framework marked "Charles Williams 2." Ovens and hearths were also made of this material. The durable soapstone held and cast the heat for hours. Soap dishes, of course, were made of soapstone. This mineral takes a high polish and is nonabsorbent.

Simple rectangles of infusible soapstone with a sturdy wire handle attached to them were heated in the fireplace or oven and used to warm the bed before retiring. Sometimes these slabs were fitted with a removable wooden or metal frame and were

Stove of soapstone in metal frame. *Courtesy Shelburne Museum, Inc.; staff photographer Einars J. Mengis*

wrapped in woolen cloths to help retain the heat. As portable warmers they were carried to church to comfort the worshiper and in later days in the wagons and sleighs to impart heat to the feet of the children on their way to school. Egg-shaped pieces of soapstone were carved to fit the hand, heated, and used as handwarmers. Other interesting pieces were carved to be used as bootwarmers and boot driers. These were heated on a hot surface or over an open flame.

Soapstone soap dish. *Courtesy Shelburne Museum, Inc.; staff photographer Einars J. Mengis*

Soapstone footwarmer with wooden case. *Courtesy Shelburne Museum, Inc.; staff photographer Einars J. Mengis*

Round and oblong griddles of soapstone were set into tight-fitting iron or copper frames with bail or side handles and retained the heat for a long time. It was not necessary to grease these griddles. A light sanding renewed the surface and removed stains. Old cooks claimed the more they were used, the better they worked. Eggs cooked on them were said to be especially flavorful.

Its heat-retaining quality led to soapstone being used for flatirons when shaped and attached to an iron handle. These were especially popular in the 1860s. Simple round slabs of soapstone were used as trivets for hot dishes and as bun warmers in baskets. They lasted for years. This pearly material was easily carved into mortars and pestles. A fascinating soapstone tobacco jar was carved circa 1840 into the form of an odd little man, his peaked cap forming the lid. It was used on the counter of the Capitol Tobacco Shop located in Concord, New Hampshire.

There are still several firms that manufacture soapstone items. One has reopened after being closed for many years. The same saws that were used 150 years ago still function. The major use of soapstone today is for chemical-proof and fire-proof table tops and sinks for laboratories. With the advent of lighter materials for making cooking utensils, soapstone was little used for such articles after the Civil War.

Soapstone tobacco jar. *Courtesy Shelburne Museum, Inc.; staff photographer Einars J. Mengis*

Storage Containers

Spices, meal, flour, sugar, salt, herbs, coffee, and tea required storage containers to keep them dry and vermin-free in the days before these foodstuffs were sold to the consumer commercially packaged. Before 1840, wooden boxes, barrels, tubs, and buckets stored cooking staples and spices in the pantry, kitchen, or cellar.

Round and oval wooden boxes were made in graduated sets or as single boxes. Stenciled letters designated the contents of each box. These hand-made boxes could be bought in the country store; some were made at home or by the local cooper (barrel maker). Finely crafted boxes are usually attributed to the Shaker or Amish religious communities. These boxes were cleverly made from strips of wood, first softened in hot water, then wrapped around a mold, lapped, and, finally, fastened with copper or iron nails or wooden pegs. The bottoms were then inserted and held in place with small nails. The lids were made in the same manner. Such boxes may be found in sizes from one inch to two feet in diameter. Sometimes oak, ash, or hickory hoops were attached to the boxes for additional strength.

Meal was stored in wooden barrels; coarse salt was kept in wooden tubs or hanging wood, pottery, pewter, or copper salt boxes. Sugar, butter, and apple butter were stored in hooped wooden buckets.

As tinplate became more plentiful, canisters and spice sets were made of it. Tin canisters, square and round, stored tea and coffee. Round and oblong tin boxes secured sets of six or seven small spice containers and often had a special slot on the inside of the lid to hold the spice grater. Most of this tinware was japanned (varnished with a hard brilliant coating) and stenciled with

226

Graduated wooden spice boxes,
brass nails

flower designs or names of the contents. There
were different-sized tin sugar and flour canisters,
bread boxes, cake boxes, and cheese boxes. This
japanned ware was very popular due to its durability, lightness, and attractiveness.

A combination flour bin and sifter of japanned
tin stored and sifted the flour. This type of round,
tin canister, ten to sixteen inches high, stored the
flour in its lidded top compartment. A hinged door
on the lower section opened on a crank-handled
sifter and a removable metal bowllike receptacle.
This flour bin-sifter could be purchased in a
twenty-, fifty-, or one-hundred-pound capacity.
Most models had removable sifters for ease in
cleaning.

Cont'd on page 232

JAPANNED COMMON CANISTERS.
TEA OR COFFEE.

Pounds,	¾	1	2	3
Per Gro..............................	10.50	16.00	24.00	30.00
Per Doz..............................	.90	1.35	2.10	2.65

CRYSTALLIZED COMMON CANISTERS.
TEA OR COFFEE.

Pounds,	¾	1	2	3
Per Gro..........................	11.50	17.00	26.00	33.00
Per Doz..........................	1.00	1.50	2.25	3.00

JAPANNED HINGED CANISTERS.
TEA OR COFFEE.

Pounds,	1	1¾	2	3	4	6
Per Gro.............	20.00	26.00	33.00	37.00	43.00	54.00
Per Doz.............	1.75	2 25	3.00	3.25	3.75	4.75

CRYSTALLIZED HINGED CANISTERS.
TEA OR COFFEE.

Pounds,	1	1¾	2	3	4	6
Per Gro.............	22.00	28.00	36.00	42.00	50.00	60.00
Per Doz.............	2.00	2.50	3.25	3.75	4.50	5.50

From U.S. Stamping Co. Catalog, Jan. 1883

From U.S. Stamping Co. Catalog, Jan. 1883

SQUARE CANISTERS.

Pounds,	2	4	6	8	12	16
Per Doz.	3.00	4.25	5.00	5.75	8.00	9.00

GROCERS' CANISTERS.

Nos.	1	2	3	4	Nest of 4.
Per Doz.	8.00	10.50	13.00	16.00	Per Nest, 3.75

FLAT TOP SUGAR BOXES.

Nos.	1	2	3	4	5	6	7	8
Inches	$4\frac{7}{8}x4\frac{7}{8}$	$5\frac{1}{2}x5\frac{3}{8}$	$6\frac{1}{8}x5\frac{3}{4}$	$7\frac{1}{4}x6\frac{7}{8}$	$8\frac{1}{4}x8\frac{1}{4}$	$10\frac{1}{2}x9\frac{1}{2}$	$11\frac{1}{4}x9\frac{3}{4}$	$13\frac{1}{4}x10\frac{7}{8}$
Per Doz.	4.00	4.50	5.50	7.00	8.00	9.50	12.00	15.00

	Nest of 4 Small.	Nest of 4 Medium.
Per Nest	1.75	2.25

	Nest of 4 Large.	Nest of 8.
Per Nest	3.00	4.50

RAISED TOP SUGAR BOXES.

Nos.	1	2	3	4	5	6
Inches	$4x3\frac{3}{4}$	$4\frac{1}{2}x5\frac{1}{8}$	$5\frac{5}{8}x5\frac{1}{2}$	$6x6\frac{1}{4}$	$7x7\frac{1}{4}$	$8x9$
Per Doz.	3.00	4.00	5.00	6.00	7.00	8.00

	Nest of 3.	Nest of 4.	Nest of 6.
Per Nest	1.00	1.40	2.75

DESK TOP SPICE BOXES.

Inches,	9¾
Per Doz..	7.50

ROUND SPICE BOXES.

Inches,	7½	8½
Per Doz...	9.00	11.00

SPICE BOXES—ROUND BOXES INSIDE.

Inches,	9¾	11½
Per Doz.........	10.00	15.00

SPICE BOXES—SQUARE BOXES INSIDE.

Inches,	9½
Per Doz	10.50

From U.S. Stamping Co. Catalog, Jan. 1883

SQUARE BREAD OR CAKE BOXES.

BROWN, OAK OR WALNUT.

Nos.	1	2	3	Nest of 3.
Inches.........	$13\frac{1}{2}$x$10\frac{1}{2}$x$9\frac{3}{4}$	15x11x$10\frac{1}{4}$	16x$12\frac{3}{4}$x$11\frac{3}{4}$	
Each.........	1.25	1.50	1.75	4.00

SQUARE BREAD OR CAKE BOXES.

CRYSTALLIZED.

Nos.	1	2	3	Nest of 3.
Inches.........	$13\frac{1}{2}$x$10\frac{1}{2}$x$9\frac{3}{4}$	15x11x$10\frac{1}{4}$	16x$12\frac{3}{4}$x$11\frac{1}{4}$	
Each.........	1.50	1.75	2.00	4.75

ROUND CAKE OR CRACKER BOXES.

BROWN, OAK OR WALNUT.

Nos.	1	2	3	Nest of 3.
Inches............	$9\frac{3}{4}$x$7\frac{3}{4}$	$10\frac{1}{2}$x9	$13\frac{1}{4}$x$9\frac{3}{4}$	
Each............	.90	1.10	1.50	Per Nest, 3.00

ROUND CAKE OR CRACKER BOXES.

CRYSTALLIZED.

Nos.	1	2	3	Nest of 3.
Inches............	$9\frac{3}{4}$x$7\frac{3}{4}$	$10\frac{1}{2}$x9	$13\frac{1}{4}$x$9\frac{3}{4}$	
Each............	1.15	1.35	1.60	Per Nest, 3.75

From U.S. Stamping Co. Catalog, Jan. 1883

ROUND CHEESE BOXES.

Nos.	1	2	Nest of 2.
Inches	$9\frac{3}{4}$x$7\frac{3}{4}$	$10\frac{1}{2}$x9	
Each	.90	1.20	Per Nest, 2.00

CAKE CLOSETS.

Nos.	1	2	3
Inches	13x10x$9\frac{1}{4}$	$15\frac{1}{2}$x$11\frac{1}{2}$x10	$17\frac{1}{2}$x$12\frac{3}{4}$x$12\frac{1}{4}$
Each	3.00	3.50	4.50

From U.S. Stamping Co. Catalog, Jan. 1883

During the Victorian era wooden spice cabinets were also used. These were hanging wooden cabinets with several small labeled drawers for storing whole peppercorns, cloves, baking powder, and other cooking ingredients. Sometimes the drawers boasted white porcelain content labels.

In the late nineteenth century canister sets were made in a variety of china and pottery patterns. Many of these were of German manufacture. Especially attractive patterns were the Meissen onion pattern and the Dutch and German Delft designs.

After the turn of the century, glass canister sets were produced. These had aluminum screw lids and came in clear and colored glass. Emerald green glass ones with a swirled rib pattern were both attractive and practical, the ribs providing a better hand grip. Silver-colored paper labels were embossed with the name of the contents.

German Meissen onion pattern
barley canister

Left to right: Swirled emerald green glass sugar container with aluminum lid; clear
ribbed glass coffee canister with aluminum lid

As foodstuffs began to come packaged in cardboard boxes, tin cans, and screw-lid jars, the variety and number of storage containers diminished. The pantry with its tubs, buckets, barrels, and canisters was no longer a necessary kitchen adjunct.

Toasters and Waffle Irons

In colonial days toasters for use by the fireplace were hand-wrought from iron. The blacksmith appreciated his own work; hence, these toasters were often embellished with curlicues, scrolls, hearts, and loops. The toasters had long handles so that the cook's hands would be well away from the heat. Some toasters had rotating heads to more efficiently complete their task; others had jointed heads which flipped to allow the toast to be browned on both sides. Some varieties were footed so that they could be set before the fire; other models had to be held in the hand.

Toasting forks with two or three tines were also used. These special forks were made of iron or heavy wire. Widely spaced tines held the bread or other foodstuff securely while it was being toasted. These, too, had long handles, and the wire ones usually had twisted shanks and tines for added strength.

In the late nineteenth century the "Lightning Bread Toaster" toasted four slices of bread in two minutes on its slanted sides and at the same time boiled tea or coffee on its flat top. This steel toaster was recommended for use on any gas, gasoline, or oil stove. The "Knoblock Pyramid Toaster," similar to the above, was patented in 1909. The Wolff Appliance Company patented the "Wolff Visible Toaster" in 1920. This toaster consisted of a steel plate with four wire frames to hold the bread in place. It was made to set over a coal-stove lid opening; it folded flat for storage.

The first electric toasters browned the bread on one side only, then the bread was manually turned so that the other side could be toasted.

Waffle and wafer irons were used in the days of fireplace cookery. These cast-iron implements had long pincerlike handles. Wafer irons had oval

From Good Housekeeping, Jan. 1921

Hand-wrought iron swiveling-head fireplace toaster

Wrought-iron toaster from Pennsylvania, eighteenth-century. *Courtesy The Metropolitan Museum of Art; gift of Mrs. Robert W. de Forest, 1933*

"Knoblock Pyramid Toaster," patented 1909

"Wolff Visible Toaster," patented 1920

Heart-Star Waffles!

Oᴺᴇ ᴡʜɪꜰꜰ ᴏꜰ ᴛʜᴏsᴇ ᴅᴇʟɪᴄɪᴏᴜs ʜᴏᴛ ᴡᴀꜰꜰʟᴇs brings the whole family to the table quick! You don't have to call them twice.

It seems as if they would never get tired of hearing those welcome words, "Have a heart!" For waffles baked crisp and evenly brown in the Griswold Heart-Star Waffle Iron, are a treat for old and young.

It's a treat you know is good for them—could anything be better than light, delicate, perfectly baked waffles, with butter and pure syrup, or wholesome jams and jelly!

For Sunday breakfast, for luncheon any day, for a chicken dinner—well, there's almost no time when good waffles aren't appropriate and welcome!

Griswold Heart-Star Waffle Irons come in two styles, No. 118, High Frame, and No. 18, Low Frame; either cast iron or aluminum pans. Also other Griswold Waffle Irons with round or square pans.

Write for booklet giving recipes and suggestions for serving waffles.

Tʜᴇ Gʀɪsᴡᴏʟᴅ Mꜰɢ. Co.
Dept. J-2, Erie, Penna., U. S. A.

Makers of the Bolo Oven, Extra Finished Iron Kitchen Ware, Heart-Star Waffle Irons, Cast Aluminum Cooking Utensils, Food Choppers, Reversible Dampers, Steel Damper Clips and Gas Hot Plates.

From Ladies' Home Journal, 1923

or round heads about six inches in diameter and engraved so that they formed raised designs on the baked wafers. Waffle irons were larger and had round or rectangular heads. Occasionally waffle irons were made with square or heart-shaped heads.

Cast-iron waffle irons for use on the coal stove sometimes had ball-and-socket joints to allow them to be turned over with greater ease. Some had pie-shaped designs or heart and star motifs on the grids. Three nineteenth-century manufacturers of these were the Fanner Manufacturing Company of Cleveland, Ohio, the Wagner Manufacturing Company of Sidney, Ohio, and the Stover Manufacturing and Engine Company of Freeport, Illinois. The Griswold Manufacturing Company of Erie, Pennsylvania, made waffle irons for the coal stove up through the 1920s. These waffle irons came in seven-, eight-, and nine-inch sizes to fit the various sizes of stove-lid openings.

"CRESCENT"
WAFFLE IRONS

WOOD HANDLES, JAPANNED BASE

Diameter, inches	7	8
"Crescent"____Per dozen	$11.00	12.00

From Biddle Hardware Co. Catalog, 1910

Trivets

A trivet is a decorative or utilitarian stand or support which serves an ornamental or useful purpose. The word "trivet" means "three feet." Many early American trivets did, indeed, have three feet, but some had more, and some had none. Some had very long legs; others had the shortest possible feet. Trivet shapes varied from triangular to round, square, oblong, oval, scalloped, and other fanciful shapes.

The most common trivet was that on which the hot sadiron was placed. The trivets were made of hand-forged iron in early America and of cast iron beginning about 1850. The hand-wrought ones were made with short legs for holding a sadiron and with higher legs in larger sizes to support pots and kettles for cooking or warming food in the fireplace. These hand-forged ones were sturdy and usually simple in structure and design. The cast-iron ones bore the names of foundries, laundry supply-houses, sadiron trade names, fraternal organizations, mottoes, likenesses

Hand-wrought-iron
fireplace trivet,
eighteenth-century

Cast-iron trivet, design called "Lantz"; mid-nineteenth-century

of famous personages, dates, letters, and numerous fanciful and lacy designs. Sizes ranged from the miniature sizes for children's toy irons to regular sadiron size to large sizes to fit the long, heavy "tailor's goose" irons. Some sadiron trivets were nickel-plated; a few rare ones had porcelain feet; a few were cast or stamped in brass. The brass ones were especially handsome.

Trivets for protecting surfaces from hot pots, dishes, and kettles were made in wire, brass, silver-plate and sterling, pressed glass and cut crystal, nickel-plate, china, pottery, and tile. The tile and glass ones were often set into metal frames. Round china and pottery trivets were popular for use under teapots in the late 1800s and early 1900s. These were customarily about six inches in diameter. Oval ones were also made. These so-called tea tiles often bore advertising and were probably "give-aways."

For decorative use only, mirrored plateaus were

Mirrored plateau, gilt
white metal rim,
nineteenth-century

produced in round shapes and in sets consisting
of oblong sections with half-round end sections.
These sets could be fitted together in various ways
to form different sizes and shapes of plateaus.
These were formal centerpiece accessories, and a
silver or cut-glass bowl elevated on a mirrored
plateau sparkled with elegance. Plateaus became
popular about 1810 and remained so until the
end of the nineteenth century.

An ingenious trivet called a "dish cross" was
used to protect the table from hot dishes or to raise
a centerpiece to best advantage. These X-shaped,
four-footed trivets, made of many metals including
brass and silver, were adjustable to fit dishes of
various sizes and shapes. Some were fitted with a
spirit lamp at the juncture of the bars to keep
foods warm at the table. Dish crosses were popular
from the late eighteenth century to the mid-nineteenth century. Fine reproductions of these are
being made today.

SADIRON STANDS.

Per Gro...6.00
Per Doz...50

COFFEE POT STANDS.

	Japanned.	Bronzed.
Per Gro..........................	6.00	7.00
Per Doz..........................	.50	.60

From U. S. Stamping Co. Catalog,
Jan. 1883

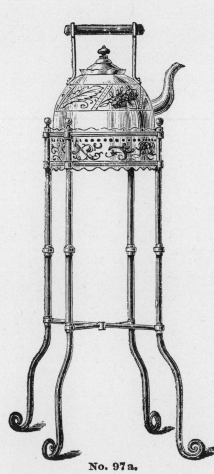

No. 97a.
Five O'clock Teakettles in variety of
shapes. Brass and Wrought Iron.

From F. A. Walker & Co. Catalog,
1886

Various trivets were employed in the ritual of the afternoon tea. Teakettle stands in a variety of shapes were made in brass and wrought iron. They stood from sixteen to thirty-six inches high and were sometimes called footmen. In the eighteenth century, teapot stands were graceful in design. In the Victorian era some were so elaborate as to appear bizarre. Brass trivets were especially constructed to hook over the edge of a fine brass fireplace fender to keep the teakettle warm. A trivet with rolling casters was conceived for the purpose of sliding a hot teapot around the table. It was called, appropriately, a "teaslider."

Easel-like slanted trivets kept a plate or two warm before the fireplace. These fireside plate warmers are quite rare today.

Stove-grate trivets and stove-pipe trivets were appurtenances for the coal stove. Stove-pipe trivets were designed to fit around the smokestack of the stove. These became popular during the Civil War. Some had removable extension shelves on which kettles of water and pots of food were set to keep warm.

Many reproductions and adaptations of the old trivets are being manufactured today. Reproductions of the old cast-iron ones are being made in both iron and aluminum.

It was the custom in the 1700s and the early 1800s to wash the family clothes and linens in a huge wooden tub placed out of doors. In the South, the separate kitchen outbuilding was also used for a laundry, or a laundry building or washhouse was built just for this purpose. The water was first heated in huge, round, iron or copper kettles over a hot fire built in the fireplace or out in the yard. A sturdy wooden stick was used to lift, push, and beat the clothes in the water. A scoopful of homemade soft soap provided the washing agent. The wash stick or washing bat was sometimes simply a plain stick or a tree branch. Artistically inclined men carved more elaborate sticks for their wives with, perhaps, even a decorative captive ring. The captive ring, adding both embellishment and additional agitation, was carved out of the same block of wood in such a way that it could not be removed. These wash sticks were used from the seventeenth century through the nineteenth century. An oar-shaped paddle was sometimes used in much the same manner to push and stir the laundry in the washtub or boiler.

Long wooden scrubbing sticks, also called mangle boards, three to six inches wide and one to two feet long, were the forerunners of the scrubbing board as we know it today. These

Washboards and Wringers

Wooden scrubbing stick, early nineteenth-century

Rockingham pottery washboard, circa 1850. *Photograph courtesy Bennington Pottery and Porcelain by Richard Carter Barret, Crown Publishers*

scrubbing sticks had corrugated grooves cut into the thick wood, and the clothes were scrubbed with them against the side of the wooden washtub. The scrubbers usually had hand holds carved into

WASH BOILERS

DIMENSIONS
No. **8**, 10¾ x 21¾ inches; No. **9**, 11½ x 23½ inches.
Black Wood Handles.

No			8	9
I C, Metallic Bottom	Per dozen		$16.00	17.00
" "	"	"	18.50	20.00
"	"	"	23.25	25.25

Quarter dozen in a Crate.

*From Biddle Hardware
Co. Catalog, 1910*

them for a better grip to scrub, squeeze, and press the wet laundry.

In the mid-1800s the wider wooden washboard with corrugated or spool-shaped wooden scrubbing surfaces came into use. A rare washboard had a wooden frame with a Rockingham pottery scrubber. This type was made circa 1850. Later, the common zinc-faced washboard, the glass washboard, and the more expensive brass washboard were manufactured on a mass scale. At about this same time the wooden washtub gave way to the tin or copper oval-shaped wash boilers which were used on the new coal ranges. Cast-iron wash boilers lined with white porcelain were also made. These were cheaper than the copper ones but more expensive than the tin. Wash boilers were also used to boil hams and in home canning.

In earliest days, the water was wrung out of the clothes by hand, later by crank-handled wringers with wooden rollers, and still later by wringers with rubber rollers. Three popular early rubber-

Cont'd on page 250

WASH BOARDS

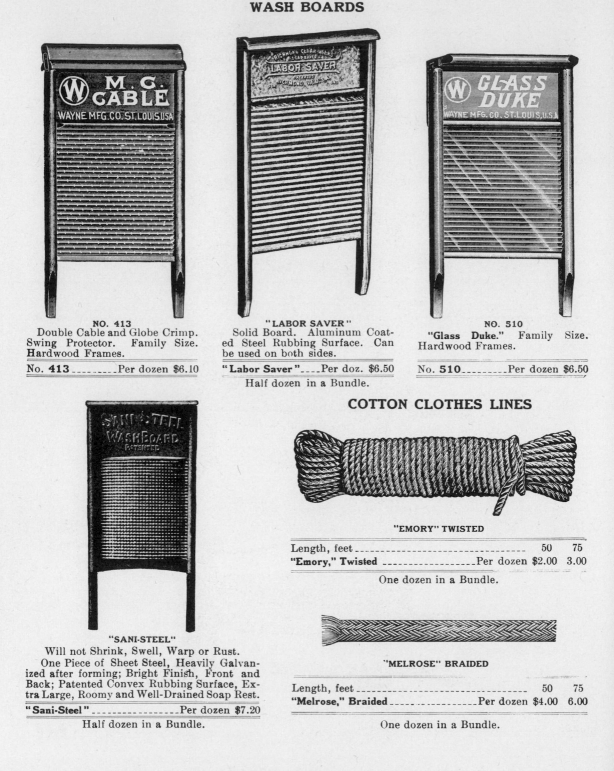

NO. 413
Double Cable and Globe Crimp. Swing Protector. Family Size. Hardwood Frames.

No. 413 _____ Per dozen $6.10

"LABOR SAVER"
Solid Board. Aluminum Coated Steel Rubbing Surface. Can be used on both sides.

"Labor Saver" ____ Per doz. $6.50

Half dozen in a Bundle.

NO. 510
"Glass Duke." Family Size. Hardwood Frames.

No. 510 _____ Per dozen $6.50

"SANI-STEEL"
Will not Shrink, Swell, Warp or Rust. One Piece of Sheet Steel, Heavily Galvanized after forming; Bright Finish, Front and Back; Patented Convex Rubbing Surface, Extra Large, Roomy and Well-Drained Soap Rest.

"Sani-Steel" _____ Per dozen $7.20

Half dozen in a Bundle.

COTTON CLOTHES LINES

"EMORY" TWISTED

Length, feet	50	75
"Emory," Twisted ____ Per dozen	$2.00	3.00

One dozen in a Bundle.

"MELROSE" BRAIDED

Length, feet	50	75
"Melrose," Braided ____ Per dozen	$4.00	6.00

One dozen in a Bundle.

From Biddle Hardware Co. Catalog, 1910

CLOTHES WRINGERS

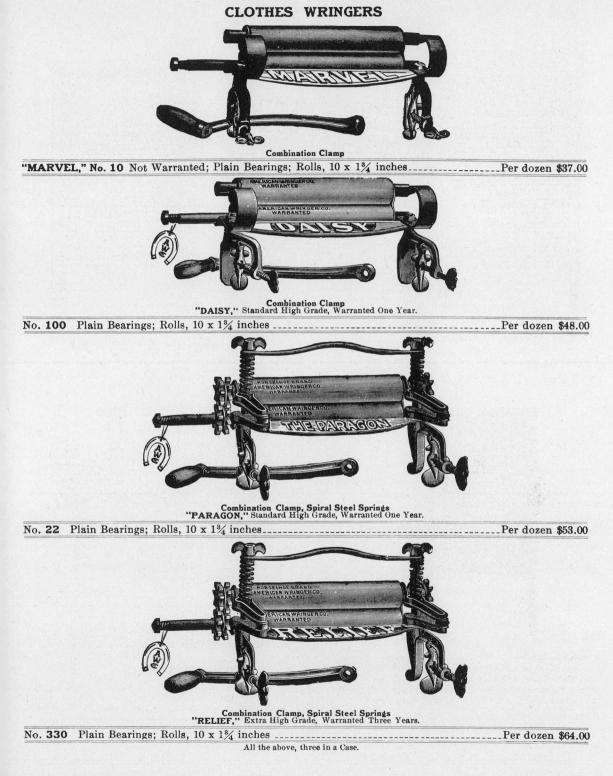

Combination Clamp

"MARVEL," No. 10 Not Warranted; Plain Bearings; Rolls, 10 x 1¾ inches ------------------ Per dozen $37.00

Combination Clamp
"DAISY," Standard High Grade, Warranted One Year.

No. 100 Plain Bearings; Rolls, 10 x 1¾ inches -------------------------------------- Per dozen $48.00

Combination Clamp, Spiral Steel Springs
"PARAGON," Standard High Grade, Warranted One Year.

No. 22 Plain Bearings; Rolls, 10 x 1¾ inches -- Per dozen $53.00

Combination Clamp, Spiral Steel Springs
"RELIEF," Extra High Grade, Warranted Three Years.

No. 330 Plain Bearings; Rolls, 10 x 1¾ inches -------------------------------------- Per dozen $64.00

All the above, three in a Case.

From Biddle Hardware Co. Catalog, 1910

roller wringers were the Universal, the Rival, and the Royal. These were all variations of the Horseshoe brand of the American Wringer Company of New York City.

In the eighteenth century, after the laundry was wrung by hand, it was hung out of doors or laid on the ground or over bushes to dry. In inclement weather a folding indoor drying rack or a long, swinging, drying rack, which swung out in front of the ever-present fire in the huge fireplace, was used. This long wooden bar was also called a clothes crane or clothes bar. Wooden stocking and, occasionally, mitten and glove driers were cut out by hand and used to shape these homemade items while they were drying. Wooden sweater stretchers were fastened together with handmade pegs and folded for storage. In 1900, a popular indoor drier was the umbrella clothes bar, a floor-standing wooden drier which opened like an umbrella. It offered thirty-two feet of drying surface for 98¢.

The first clothespins were carved by hand, sometimes in the quaint shapes of people. These first pins were sturdy and large, six inches or longer, to hold the heavy homespun linens on the thick hemp clotheslines. Unusual whalebone

Cont'd on page 255

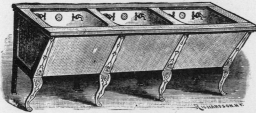

WASHING MACHINES

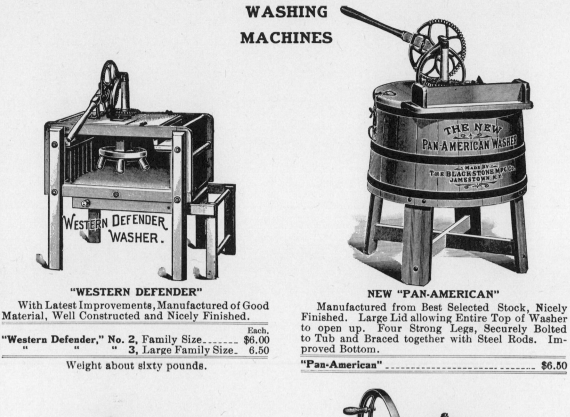

"WESTERN DEFENDER"

With Latest Improvements, Manufactured of Good Material, Well Constructed and Nicely Finished.

	Each.
"Western Defender," No. 2, Family Size	$6.00
" " " 3, Large Family Size	6.50

Weight about sixty pounds.

NEW "PAN-AMERICAN"

Manufactured from Best Selected Stock, Nicely Finished. Large Lid allowing Entire Top of Washer to open up. Four Strong Legs, Securely Bolted to Tub and Braced together with Steel Rods. Improved Bottom.

"Pan-American"	$6.50

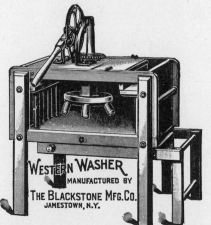

"WESTERN," NEW IMPROVED

With Sliding Rack for Tub and Improved Drop End Handles.

	Each.
"Western," No. 2, Family Size	$7.00
" " 3, Large Family Size	7.50

Weight about sixty pounds.

"IMPERIAL" ROTARY

Built with Sliding Cylinder on Square Post, insuring great strength. It has Roller Bearings, thereby making it, when loaded with clothes, practically noiseless.

"Imperial" Rotary	Each $10.50

Weight about seventy pounds.

From Biddle Hardware Co. Catalog, 1910

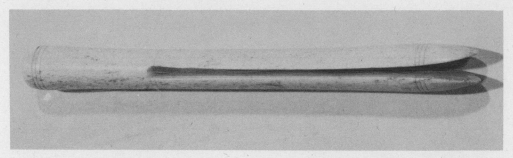

Carved whalebone clothespin. *Courtesy Mystic Seaport; photo by Louis S. Martel*

FIRST CLASS CLOTHES PINS.

18 cts. gross.

*From Van Heusen-Charles Co.
Catalog, 1898*

*From Munsey's Magazine, Feb.
1899*

CLOTHES WRINGERS

"NOVELTY"
Extra High Grade
Warranted 3 Years.

"NOVELTY"
Extra High Grade
Warranted 3 Years.

Selected Hard Maple, Blue Wood Spring, Red Steel Spring

PLAIN BEARINGS			BALL BEARINGS			PLAIN BEARINGS			FOR ROUND OR SQUARE TUBS		
No.	Rolls, inches.	Per doz.	No.	Rolls, inches.	Per doz.	No.	Rolls, inches.	Per doz.	No.	Rolls, inches.	Per doz.
300	10 x 1¾	$64.00	390	10 x 1¾	$71.00	337	10 x 1¾	$66.00	371	11 x 1¾	$73.00
301	11 x 1¾	71.00	391	11 x 1¾	78.00	338	11 x 1¾	73.00			
302	12 x 1¾	78.00				339	12 x 1¾	80.00			

"EMPIRE"
Extra High Grade   Warranted 3 Years.

"ROYAL"
Highest Grade
Warranted 5 Years.

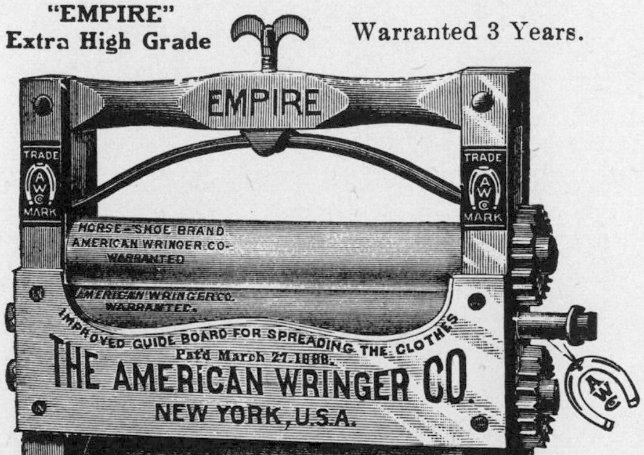

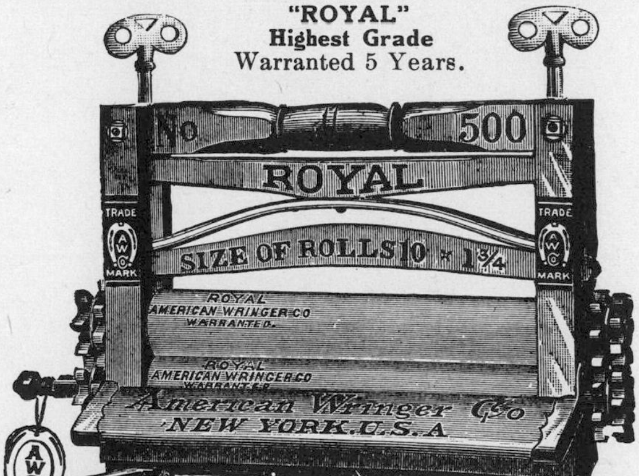

Purchase Gear, Brass Bushing on Crank Journal
Natural Wood Finish, Galvanized Spring.

Hard Maple Frame, Blue Wood Spring, Red Steel Spring

PLAIN BEARINGS						PLAIN BEARINGS					
No.	Rolls, inches.	Per doz.	No.	Rolls, inches.	Per doz.	No.	Rolls, inches.	Per doz.	No.	Rolls, inches.	Per doz.
300	10 x 1¾	$70.00	305	12 x 1⅞	$95.00	500	10 x 1¾	$75.00	504	11 x 1⅞	$94.00
301	11 x 1¾	77.00				501	11 x 1¾	83.00	505	12 x 1⅞	105.00

All the above, three in a Case.

WASHING MACHINES

The Snowball is a Rotary Washer different from other Machines, because the Driving Mechanism is entirely enclosed in a Ball. It is impossible for children to get their fingers and hands caught in the Gears. Solidly Built of Best Material, Light Running and Practical. Improved Telescope Drive and Galvanized Dasher. This Galvanized Dasher has a Cypress Bottom and Wood Pins. This is improved and so constructed that the Centre Post or Drive is telescopic, therefore it does not crowd and push the clothes away from the Pins in the Dasher when washing. There is no slipping and winding on any Centre Post in this Washer. The Driving Mechanism Reverses by a Clutch having Case-Hardened Steel Spools. The Fly Wheel has Two Lugs and the Handle can be easily changed to give High Speed or Regular Speed. The touch of a simple Bessemer Steel Fastener attaches and removes the Fly Wheel in an instant. An Automatic Lid Lock locks the Machine firmly.

"Snowball" --Each $11.00

Weight about seventy pounds.

"SNOWBALL"

"MISSION"

With Folding Hardwood Bench Braced with Steel Braces which furnishes a Convenient Stand for the Clothes Basket or Rinsing Tub and a strong solid support for the Wringer. The Tub swings in one direction on Hardened Steel Ball Bearings and the Inside Rubber or Dasher turns in the opposite, thereby cleansing the clothes in the shortest possible time. The Machine is supplied with Two Powerful Steel Springs placed underneath the Tub, which perform nearly all the work, just a little help being required from the operator at each swing. All Inside Castings are Galvanized. No chance for rust to get on the clothes.

"Mission" ------------------------------Each $12.50

Weight about one hundred pounds.

"WINCHESTER"

High Speed Fly Wheel, Fast Revolving Dasher

Neat in design and construction. Double thickness overlap Lid. When open allows plenty of room for operator to put in and take out clothes.

Large Tub made of Louisiana Red Cypress. Plenty of room for large-sized Wringer. The Dasher is fitted with a new device for preventing clothes from catching and tearing. The Castings are so balanced that by lifting with the Lever, the Cover will open very easily.

The Castings, where extra strength is required, are made malleable, insuring against breakage.

It runs quietly and embodies the desired high speed with the least possible effort.

"Winchester" --------------------Each $12.50

Weight about eighty-five pounds.

From Biddle Hardware Co. Catalog, 1910

clothespins were carved by sailors on their long sea voyages and presented to their wives and sweethearts. These were one-of-a-kind, and their embellishment depended on the skill and imagination of the whittler. Manufactured clothespins became standard goods toward the end of the nineteenth century. These factory-made clothespins, both the standard push-on type and the spring-clip type, have remained almost unchanged to this day.

Wedgwood Kitchenware

Everyone is familiar with the beautiful decorative wares of Josiah Wedgwood and his successors, but few are as well acquainted with his useful wares. Wedgwood produced many pieces of practical pottery for the preparing of food. These pieces were, of course, made in England, but many found their way to America via colonists, visitors, and merchants.

Molds for aspic, butter, and jelly were produced in cream-colored Queen's Ware and in glazed Pearlware, the fish-shaped ones being especially attractive. Wedge-shaped and round covered cheese dishes went from kitchen to table. Octagonal molds with artistically pierced designs were lined with cheesecloth and filled with cream and curds which gradually solidified into a block of mild cheese. Soft custard was contained in and poured from an elliptical blue and white Jasper custard cup. Boiled eggs were held in smooth Caneware egg hoops, a type of open-end egg cup. Another accessory for eggs was a Queen's Ware teaspoon used for eating eggs. The egg would not tarnish this pottery spoon as it would a silver one.

A spoon-shaped gadget with a short handle and perforated bowl was an egg separator. The white of the egg flowed through the holes, but the yolk

Queen's Ware fish mold, 1800. *Courtesy Buten Museum of Wedgwood*

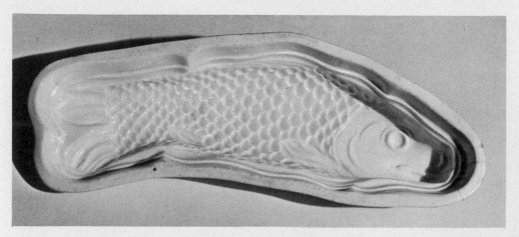

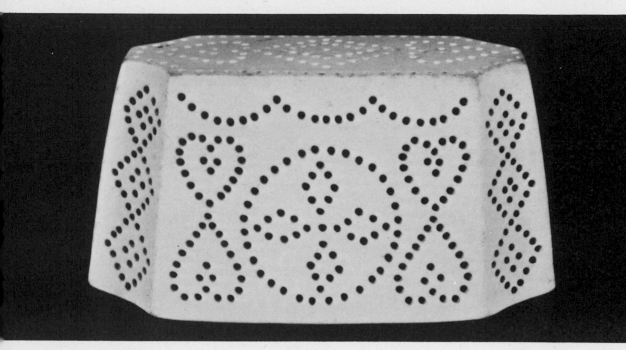

Queen's Ware cheese mold, 1790. *Courtesy Buten Museum of Wedgwood*

Assorted Queen's Ware and Pearlware molds, nineteenth-century. *Courtesy Buten Museum of Wedgwood*

Queen's Ware egg
separator, 1800. *Courtesy
Buten Museum of
Wedgwood*

remained in the bowl. This very modern looking piece of kitchenware was made in 1780.

A wide-bladed fish server was decoratively pierced in a snowflake pattern. A long-spouted Queen's Ware funnel, shaped like a lotus flower, was a study in functional simplicity. Six white Jasper measuring cups in a graduated set were probably made for a chemist, but any cook would have loved to have them in her kitchen. This was also true of a stoneware mortar and pestle designed in 1779. "Hot plates" were almost a necessity in the days when kitchens were sometimes far from the dining room, often in a separate outbuilding. Hot water, poured through a large center hole into the hollow innards of the "hot plate," kept warm the dinner plate on the top.

Pearlware invalid feeder,
1810. *Courtesy Buten
Museum of Wedgwood*

Queen's Ware night nurse to keep
gruel warm by the sick bed, 1850.
*Courtesy Buten Museum of
Wedgwood*

For the feeding of the invalid and infant, a
pap-feeder was designed in decorated Pearlware.
Liquid and semi-liquid foods were fed through
the wide spout. A teapot-shaped baby-feeder, circa
1810, had a long, narrow spout, ending in a nipple
with perforations. A more elegant infant-feeder
would be difficult to find. A nineteenth-century
physic cup was used to dispense liquid medicine.
The handle was in the fanciful form of a dog's
head. A "night nurse" or "veilleuse" kept gruel
warm at the bedside of an invalid.

Dairy accessories included a "dairy open cup,"
a settling pan, and a 14½-inch-long skimmer
spoon. The "dairy open cup," so called because it
looked like a bottomless cup, was used as a funnel.
A rim around the bottom opening permitted the
binding of a screen, such as cheesecloth, to strain
foreign matter from the milk. The oval shallow
settling pan allowed the cream to rise to the sur-

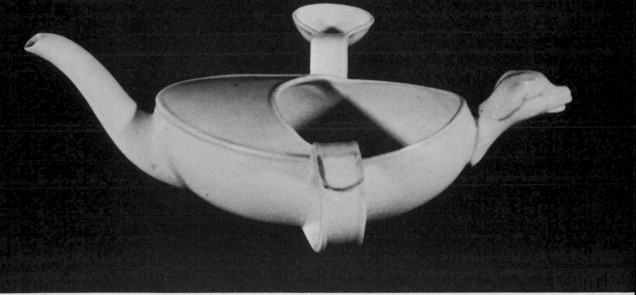

Queen's Ware physic cup, nineteenth-century. *Courtesy Buten Museum of Wedgwood*

Baby feeder, 1810, underglaze blue; perforated nipple. *Courtesy Buten Museum of Wedgwood*

face where it could be easily skimmed off with the skimmer spoon or a Queen's Ware perforated skimmer. These have been found marked with the dairy name and crest.

A laundry aid made by Wedgwood was a pair of five-inch-high Queen's Ware sock forms. Young children's socks were stretched on these to retain their shape while hastening their drying.

The pungent flavor of watercress was enjoyed in 1870. It appeared on the table in diamond-shaped perforated watercress dishes of Pearlware. Pearlware cruet sets consisted of dispensers for oil, vinegar, mustard, salt, and pepper. Platter tilters in an underglaze blue decoration were unusual items. Wider at one edge, they were placed under platters, and their tilted position then allowed the gravy to flow to one side. A plain, white, glazed double-boiler had a tinned steel handle and cover. It was probably the most primitive-looking piece Wedgwood ever made. Argyles were intriguingly shaped vessels for keeping gravy warm. Hot water was poured into the lower of the two compartments. These oddities, as Wedgwood designed them, had one handle and two spouts.

Bar accessories, such as liquor labels and wine-bottle coasters, were also created by the talented Wedgwood.

Cont'd on page 264

Queen's Ware wine funnel with inside strainer, 1790. *Courtesy Buten Museum of Wedgwood*

Queen's Ware dairy skimmer spoon. *Courtesy Buten Museum of Wedgwood*

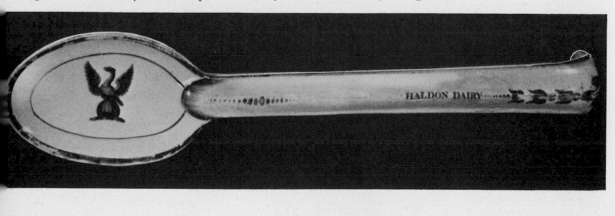

Platter tilter, 1820; underglaze blue rose decoration. *Courtesy Buten Museum of Wedgwood*

White glazed double broiler, 1875; tinplated steel handle and cover. *Courtesy Buten Museum of Wedgwood*

Pearlware cruet set, 1800. *Courtesy Buten Museum of Wedgwood*

Argyles (gravy warmers) which hold gravy in upper chamber and hot water in lower compartment, 1800. *Courtesy Buten Museum of Wedgwood*

PORT

CHERRY, BRANDY

Earthenware and Jasper bottle labels and a perforated wine coaster. *Courtesy Buten Museum of Wedgwood*

All of these articles were produced prior to 1925. Decorative or useful, old or new, Wedgwood is a thing of beauty and admiration.

W ire, a thread of metal, may be made of iron, steel, gold, silver, platinum, copper, brass, or other metals. Articles made of wire are called wire goods or wirework. Wire goods were made in the Colonies as early as the mid-seventeenth century. During this period wire potato or vegetable boilers for fireplace cookery were made, as were the brushlike wire for wooden-backed wool cards used in the making of wool yarn. Sterling, gold, and silver-on-copper wire goods were made in the eighteenth century almost exclusively in the form of jewelry and bibelots.

Wire Goods

Wire goods became big business in the middle of the nineteenth century, and whole catalogs were printed of the hundreds of items made of iron or steel wirework for kitchenware use. Many pieces were utilitarian, such as the dish drainers, potato mashers, rug beaters, vegetable washers, tea and coffee strainers, and egg boilers. Pot chains were made of a series of connected tin-plated wire circles and were used for cleaning pots and kettles, being especially effective on the old cast-iron pots. Pitchfork-shaped wire pie lifters, with or without wooden handles, removed the hot pies and cakes from the still hotter coal stoves of this era.

There were hinged wire-mesh tea or coffee balls, forerunners of the modern tea bags. Round, decorative wire stands served as trivets for hot dishes and pots. Corrugated wire broilers were made for the specific purpose of cooking oysters. Oysters were very much a part of nineteenth-century menus. A favorite method of cooking the oysters was broiling. Following is a recipe from the 1896 edition of the famous *Boston Cooking-School Cook Book* by Fannie Merritt Farmer:

Cont'd on page 270

CORRUGATED WIRE BROILERS.
LIGHT.

Nos.	0	1	2	3	4
Inches....	6x9	8x9	10x9	12x9	14x10
Per Doz....................	2.50	2.75	3.00	3.25	3.50

HEAVY.

Nos.	0	1	2	3	4
Inches....	6x9	8x9	10x9	12x9	14x10
Per Doz....................	3.00	3.50	4.00	5.00	6.00

EXTRA HEAVY.

Nos.	0	1	2	3	4
Inches................. ..	6x9	8x9	10x9	12x9	14x10
Per Doz	4.50	5.50	6.50	7.50	8.50

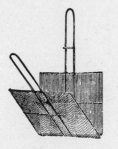

CORRUGATED WIRE OYSTER BROILERS.

Nos.	0	1	2	3	4
Inches...................	6x9	8x9	10x9	12x9	14x
Per Doz..................	5.00	6.00	7.00	8.00	9.00

CORN POPPERS.

	Square (Wire or Tin Lids.)	Round
Per Gro........................20.00		21.00
Per Doz........................ 1.75		2.00

EXTRA SIZES.

Nos.	6	7	8	9
Quarts..........	1	2	4	8
Per Doz.......................	2.00	3.00	8.00	20.

TEA OR COFFEE STRAINERS.

	Nos. 5, Plain.	8, Solid Rim.	8, Solid Rim, Silver Plated.
Inches	$1\frac{3}{4}$	$1\frac{3}{4}$	$1\frac{3}{4}$
Per Doz	1.25	1 75	3.00

TEA OR COFFEE BALLS.

Nos.	1	2	3	4
Inches	$1\frac{3}{4}$	$2\frac{1}{8}$	$2\frac{1}{2}$	$2\frac{7}{8}$
Per Doz	.2.50	3.50	4.50	5.50

WIRE HANDLE STRAINERS.

Nos.	1	2	3
Inches	$2\frac{1}{4}$	$3\frac{1}{8}$	$3\frac{7}{8}$
Per Doz	.2.50	3.00	4.00

WOOD HANDLE STRAINERS.

Nos.	1	2	3
Inches	$2\frac{1}{2}$	$3\frac{1}{8}$	$3\frac{7}{8}$
Per Doz	.2.75	3.25	4.25

SHERWOOD'S TEA OR COFFEE POT STANDS.

Nos.	1	3
Inches	6	7
Per Doz	.1.75	2.50

NATIONAL TEA OR COFFEE POT STANDS.

Per Gro	13.50
Per Doz	1.20

From U.S. Stamping Co. Catalog, 1886

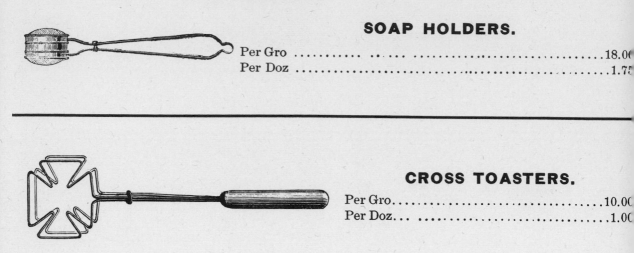

SOAP HOLDERS.

Per Gro 18.00

Per Doz 1.75

CROSS TOASTERS.

Per Gro...................................10.00

Per Doz... ....1.00

HOME HEATING RACKS.

PATENTED.

Per Doz., with Cup................ ....2.00

A very convenient article for heating water over any kind of kerosene lamp.

From U.S. Stamping Co. Catalog, 1886

From Iron Age, Jan. 9, 1890

From U.S. Stamping Co. Catalog, 1886

FLY TRAPS.

	Harper's,	Peerless.	Balloon.
Per Doz.......... ....3.00	3.00	2.75

CONDUCTOR STRAINERS.

Inches,	2	3	4	5	6
Per Doz........ ....2.50	3.00	3.50	4.00	4.50

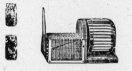

WHEEL MOUSE TRAPS.

Per Doz.... ....2.50

CAM RAT TRAPS—RETINNED.

Inches,	6x11
Per Doz.....	3.75

VEGETABLE SKIMMERS.
WOOD HANDLE.

Per Gro...10.00

Per Doz.. 1.00

ROUND WIRE DISH COVERS.
BLUE OR TINNED.

Inches,	6	7	8	9	10	12	14	Set of 5.
Per Doz......	1.20	1.45	1.75	2.10	2.50	4.50	6.00	Per Set, .75
								(6 to 10 inch.)

OVAL WIRE DISH COVERS.
BLUE OR TINNED.

Inches,	8	10	12	14	16	18	Set of 6.
Per Doz........	2.00	3.00	4.00	5.00	6.00	7.00	Per Set, 2.25

From Van Heusen-Charles Co. Catalog, 1898

BROILED OYSTERS

1 pint selected oysters   ¼ cup melted butter
⅔ cup seasoned cracker crumbs

Clean oysters and dry between towels. Lift with plated fork by the tough muscle and dip in butter, then in cracker crumbs which have been seasoned with salt and pepper. Place in a buttered wire broiler and broil over a clear fire until juices flow, turning while broiling. Serve with or without Maitre d'Hôtel Butter.

Round and square cornpoppers with wire or tin lids were a popular item. Round or oval fine wire domes with a knob at the top served as dish and food covers in the days before window screens and flyspray were common. These came in sizes from six to eighteen inches in diameter and could be purchased in sets of graduated sizes.

Three popular wire flytraps were Harper's, Peerless, and Balloon. Rattraps and mousetraps were also manufactured in this versatile material. Inexpensive, wooden-handled ladles with open-work wire bowls were used to lift vegetables from pot-au-feu or their cooking juices. Round, square, or oblong wire soap-holders with double wire handles held closed with a sliding clasp could be swished through the water to make suds for dish-washing. They allowed tiny scraps of soap to be used and so were called soap-savers.

A quaint item was a wire toast-holder with a wooden handle. It was called a "cross toaster" because the wire which held the bread left an untoasted design in the shape of a Formée cross. A patented item that was considered a very convenient article in 1883 was called a "home heating-rack." It was a sort of tall trivet which fitted over any standing kerosene lamp and came equipped with a small pan for heating water over the lamp.

More decorative articles made in ornate patterns of wirework included epergnes, compotes, cake stands, holders for canister sets, wine-bottle-holders, and, of course, baskets. Intriguing items were fancy round wire baskets which could be folded into different designs and collapsed flat to serve as whimsical trivets. Plain or fancy, wire goods were interesting items which faded away with the nineteenth century.

From Van Heusen-Charles Co. Catalog, 1898

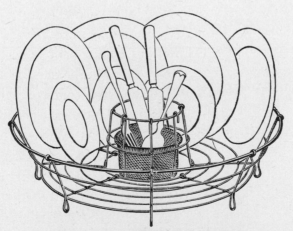

THE O. K. DISH DRAINER

Is an invaluable aid in dish washing, and only needs to be used to be appreciated.

50 cts.

Kitchenware Care

A variety of materials are represented in a collection of old kitchenware. It is important to know how to care for the different materials in order to preserve them and to display them at their best. If you actually use your old kitchen utensils, then you must give them particular attention as both the preservation of your kitchenware and the protection of your health are involved. Most of the materials of which old kitchenware was made are quite durable, but they do require some basic care to sustain them in their best condition. The following basic items are necessary for kitchenware care: fine steel wool, soap-filled steel-wool pads, scouring powder, baking soda, cream of tartar, household ammonia, salad oil, a soft brush, a stiff bristled brush, and a wire brush. All these supplies are inexpensive and readily available.

Aluminum

To brighten and remove discoloration, polish aluminum with steel-wool soap pads. Rub in one direction only. Spun aluminum pieces should be rubbed in the direction of the surface lines. The insides of pots darkened by alkaline foods may be brightened by boiling in them one quart of water to which two teaspoons of cream of tartar have been added. Boil ten minutes. Cream of tartar may be purchased in the spice department of most food stores. Lime deposits from hard water may be removed by boiling a solution of equal amounts of water and vinegar in the pot and allowing this mixture to remain in the pot overnight. Then polish with a steel-wool soap pad, wash, rinse, and dry.

Hornware

Wash with warm, sudsy water. Dry. Do not soak horn or horn-handled articles in hot water as this softens the horn and loosens cemented-on horn handles.

Iron

Rust is the arch enemy of ironware. Wrought-iron resists rust better than cast iron. Soak badly rusted articles in kerosense for twenty-four hours. Next, briskly rub off the loosened rust with a steel-wool pad. A brass-bristled brush will work more efficiently on pieces with embossed or raised designs. A steel-bristled brush may be used on large, heavy articles. Modern commercial rust removers are very efficient. After the rust has been completely removed, scrub the iron article with a stiff brush, using hot sudsy water with a few drops of disinfectant, until it is thoroughly cleaned. Towel dry and then let completely dry in the open air. Dry thoroughly or it will rust again. When absolutely dry, coat lightly with salad oil. This procedure applies to all iron cooking utensils.

To preserve cooking pots and to forestall future rusting, coat generously with vegetable oil, linseed oil, olive oil, or unsalted fat. Heat the coated article in a 250-degree oven for two hours. The iron will absorb most of the oil or fat. Apply more oil as it becomes absorbed during the heating process. When this seasoning is completed, allow the utensil to cool and wipe off the excess oil with paper towels. Repeat as often as necessary.

Occasional reappearances of rust may be removed with scouring powder and a stiff brush or a steel-wool soap pad, after which the utensil

must be re-oiled. Store pots with the lids off to prevent the formation of rust and a musty odor. Tines on old forks and the blades of iron mincing knives may be sharpened. Keep these, too, lightly oiled to stave off undesirable rust.

All pieces that are actually in use cannot, of course, be painted dull black or rubbed with black shoe polish as pieces intended for display only may be. However, it is preferable that articles be kept in their original condition as much as possible.

To store iron utensils for a long time, take certain precautions. Coat them thickly with salad oil, boiled linseed oil, petroleum jelly, unsalted fat, or paraffin, wrap in paper, and store in a dry place.

If tiny, black specks appear in food cooked in the iron pots, the vessel was not seasoned thoroughly, or it is time to reseason it. Use the same oil treatment in a slow oven as mentioned above.

The basic rules for the care of ironware are: keep clean; dry thoroughly; keep oiled.

Collection of woodenware and ironware: *Left to right, top shelf*: Quassia cup; large salt shaker or sugar shaker; huge mortar and pestle; small masher; wood and iron coffee-grinder; toddy stick; plain Shaker masher; family-size wooden trencher in back. *Second shelf:* Two-part fluting iron; balance scale; sadiron; two round chopping boards standing at back. *Third shelf, hanging:* Iron lemon squeezer; iron ice pick; iron pot scraper; hand-forged iron food chopper; cast-iron bottle opener; iron ice pick; steel olive fork. *On third shelf:* Star butter mold; oblong cheese box; Pennsylvania Dutch tulip butter stamp. *Hanging from bottom shelf:* butter paddle; stirring paddle; wooden tea strainer; meat tenderizer; double-bladed slaw cutter; lemon squeezer; three-pronged fork; mixing paddle; hand-carved deep bowl spoon. *Hanging on wall:* Small scoops, mashers, shaping paddles, cookie prints. *Photo by Willafred*

NICKELWARE

Nickel-plated articles require little care. They should be washed in hot sudsy water, towel dried, and then gently polished to a shine with a soft towel or flannel cloth. Especially soiled or greasy spots may be rubbed lightly with a damp cloth and a small amount of cleanser. A final wiping off with alcohol, which evaporates quickly, will leave a smudgeless shine. Nickelware in bad condition may be replated.

To remove rust spots in nickel-plate, cover spot with oil or grease, let set several days, then rub with cloth soaked in ammonia. This will remove the rust without harming the nickel-plate. Wash, dry well, and polish.

Nickel silver or German silver may be made to shine by rubbing with a soap-filled steel-wool pad. Then polish with a good silver polish. Do not put nickel silver articles in the automatic dishwasher as the dishwasher detergents will give the metal a greenish cast almost impossible to remove.

PEWTER

Most antique collectors prefer a dark, mellow finish on their old pieces of pewter. To maintain such a finish, all that is needed is a regular wiping off with a soft, dry cloth. Occasionally such pieces may be polished with any good silver polish and dried thoroughly with a soft terry towel. The less pewter pieces are handled between polishings, the fewer polishings they will need as finger marks accelerate the darkening process. Nothing compares to the rich, mellow beauty of a piece of time-darkened pewter.

Some collectors prefer that the sheen on their old pewter rival the luster of their silverware. To achieve such a gleam requires some work and considerable care. Most dealers and collectors find the lye bath the best method for brightening badly oxidized old pewter. Wash your pewter pieces well in hot detergent suds first. In a large enameled pot, dissolve one cup lye in 3 quarts of boiling water. The article must be completely covered by this solution. Lye is a caustic agent and extreme caution must be exercised in its use; wear rubber gloves, and use tongs when handling the articles being cleaned. Goggles are recommended. Allow the article to boil gently in the lye solution. Every 15 minutes remove article from solution and examine progress. When desired finish is obtained, rinse thoroughly with warm water and polish with very fine .0000 steel wool and a silver polish or one of the new special pewter polishes. Rinse again and wipe dry. Whether with a bright shine or a gentle sheen, old pewter is a thing of beauty.

Brass and Copper

Old copper and brass pieces both require the same general care. If the pieces are lacquered and are purely ornamental, then the only care necessary is that they be dusted frequently and gently to prevent scratches in the lacquer coating. Such scratches would allow the metal to tarnish. A light coating of wax will further protect the lacquer finish. If lacquered pieces become greasy, as they occasionally do when displayed in a kitchen, a careful gentle washing with a soft cloth in warm suds is permissible. Should you desire to remove this lacquer coating, it may be accomplished by soaking the article in approximately two gallons of water in which one cup of washing soda has been dissolved. After soaking the article in this mixture for twenty minutes, the coating can be peeled off.

There is an excellent brass and copper paste-type polish on the market which cleans and polishes most efficiently and leaves a protective anti-tarnish finish on the article as well. It is applied with its own little sponge. Small corroded spots may be removed with the finest steel wool and gentle rubbing. Many people prefer the darker, brownish tones of an unpolished piece of copper to the pink glow of a polished piece—both are attractive.

TIN

All old tinware was actually tin-plated; sheets of iron were coated with pure tin to prevent the iron from rusting. Therefore, tinware should not be severely scoured or scratched as the tin coating will then be damaged, allowing the iron underneath to rust. Accumulated grease may be removed by soaking the piece in one quart of water in which one-fourth cup of washing soda has been dissolved. If there are rust spots which must be scoured off, do so as gently as possible. Cooks in the know say, "darkened tins cook better pies," so do not feel obligated to make your tinware sparkle. Soak off burned foods rather than scouring them off.

Collection of tinware: *Left to right, top shelf:* Three measures; hanging match holder; bread pan; muffin tin dated 1874; small, deep pie pan. *Second shelf:* Hand-made shielded candleholder; breadstick pan; hand-punched vegetable grater; factory-made grater; corrugated chopper; two hanging hinged-top nutmeg graters; Edgar nutmeg grater, two solid-back cookie cutters. *Third shelf:* Three fluted-rim cake pans; a small coffeepot with heavy copper bottom; a funnel for filling canning jars; a smaller funnel advertising C. D. Kenny Co. (an old Maryland grocer); a fish-shaped aspic mold; a hanging salt box. *Bottom shelf:* Graceful twelve-hole candlemold; covered bail-handled lard pail; a deep, heavy cake pan with tapering sides, sometimes called a "corn pone pan"; a stirring spoon; three pie pans, the first advertises the Baltimore Pie Bakery last listed in City Directories in 1911; tin extinguisher; "hog-scraper" candlestick, Dietz lantern. *Photo by Willafred*

Most old pieces of tinware have a thicker coating of tin than their modern-day counterparts, but they should still be treated gently. Very badly rusted pieces of old tin-plate may be painted and decorated, but this procedure does detract from the original charm of their usefulness. Never use lye to clean tins as it will ruin them. Tinware, as ironware, should be thoroughly dried before being stored. Wipe as dry as possible and then place in the open air or a warm oven to dry completely.

GRANITEWARE

Graniteware was an enameled coating on an iron base. Care should be taken not to scratch or chip the enameled finish as the iron base will then be exposed to rust. Burned foods can be loosened by putting a solution of one teaspoonful of baking soda and water into the utensil and allowing the solution to boil for fifteen minutes. Then a gentle rubbing should remove the residue. If the graniteware is actually used for cooking purposes, a good idea is to rub the bottom of the pans with soap before placing over the burner of the stove. Then the bottoms of the utensils are very easy to clean. Graniteware generally requires little care due to its slick, hard enamel coating.

SOAPSTONE

Most cooking utensils made of soapstone have iron handles or frames, which should be treated as suggested in the section on iron. Soapstone requires little care as it will not corrode and is non-absorbent. It will take a high polish and responds well to an occasional rubbing with steel wool and ordinary household cleanser. It may also be cleaned by rubbing with salt and a coarse cloth. A light sanding restores the original color.

Glass and Pottery

A thorough washing with a soft brush in hot, soapless detergent is usually all the care articles made of glass and pottery require. Glassware which has contained milk should first be rinsed in cold water to prevent a cloudy residue. Stains and cloudiness may be removed from glassware by filling the articles with a solution of two teaspoons of ammonia added to warm water. After soaking several hours, empty out the solution and wash and rinse the glass as usual. Glassware washed in a soapless detergent may be left to air dry after being rinsed in hot water. Glassware washed in soap should be thoroughly rinsed and then towel dried to prevent streaking. Stains in pottery may be removed by soaking in a solution of two tablespoons of chlorine bleach and one cup of water. Let soak thirty minutes and then wash thoroughly.

Wood

Woodenware was also called "treenware" from the name of its origin, the tree. The care of old woodenware is quite simple. First scrub the article thoroughly with a stiff-bristled brush and warm, sudsy water to which a few drops of an efficient household disinfectant have been added. *Absolutely do not soak.* Woodenware will warp out of shape if allowed to get soaking wet. Scrub quickly, but thoroughly. Place on wire racks, such as cake-cooling racks, set in the bottom of the sink. Quickly pour boiling water over the woodenware. This sterilizes the articles and hastens their drying. Leave the articles on the wire racks in the open air, outdoors in the sun if possible, to dry completely and quickly. When absolutely dry, rub utensils, such as ladles, forks, and spoons, briskly with a clean cloth soaked in salad oil. The articles may first be very lightly sanded if rough or splintery. Allow the oil to penetrate for ten minutes; apply a second coat; let soak another ten minutes; now completely polish away all excess oil with a clean cloth.

Wooden bowls and trenchers may be finished with a thin coating of melted, harmless beeswax or of paraffin wax such as is used in home canning. The wax is heated until just melted in a tin can set in a pan of boiling water. Use caution as wax is inflammable. Carefully pour the melted wax over the article so as to coat it completely and evenly with a thin layer of the protective wax.

After this initial treatment, treenware will require only an occasional re-oiling or rewaxing. Bowls, mortars and pestles, and slicing boards will need only to be wiped clean after use. More heavily soiled items, such as ladles, spoons, and forks, may be quickly washed in warm running water. If it should be necessary to scrub them, re-oil them afterwards. To remove the odors of onions, garlic, etc., from your shredders, bowls, or mortars, wash them quickly in baking soda dissolved in warm water.

Bibliography

Books and Pamphlets

American Agriculturist Family Cyclopaedia. New York: American Agriculturist, 1888.

American Heritage Cookbook. New York: American Heritage Publishing Company, Inc., 1964.

America's Arts and Skills. Life Editors. New York: E. P. Dutton & Company, Inc., 1957.

BARRET, RICHARD CARTER. *Bennington Pottery and Porcelain.* New York: Crown Publishers, Inc., 1958.

BULLOCK, HELEN. *The Williamsburg Art of Cookery.* Williamsburg, Virginia: Colonial Williamsburg, Inc., 1938.

BUTEN, HARRY M. *Wedgwood Counterpoint.* Merion, Pennsylvania: The Buten Museum of Wedgwood, 1962.

CHAMPLIN, JOHN D., JR. *The Young Folks Cyclopaedia of Common Things.* New York: Henry Holt & Company, 1882.

CHRISTENSEN, ERWIN O. *The Index of American Design.* New York: Macmillan Company, 1950.

COLE, ANN KILBORN. *Antiques: How to Identify, Buy, Sell, Refinish, and Care for Them.* New York: David McKay Company, Inc., 1957.

————. *The Golden Guide to American Antiques.* New York: Golden Press, Inc., 1967.

CROWEN, T. J. *The American Lady's System of Cookery.* Auburn, New York: Derby and Miller, 1850.

DAVIDSON, MARSHALL B. *The American Heritage History of Colonial Antiques.* New York: American Heritage Publishing Company, Inc., 1967.

DREPPERD, CARL W. *A Dictionary of American Antiques.* Boston: Charles T. Branford Company, 1952.

————, AND MARJORIE M. SMITH. *Handbook of Tomorrow's Antiques.* New York: Thomas Y. Crowell Company, 1953.

EARLE, ALICE MORSE. *Home Life in Colonial Days.* New York: Macmillan Company, 1898.

EGGLESTON, EDWARD. *Stories of American Life and Adventure.* New York: American Book Company, 1895.

Finishes for Alcoa Aluminum. Pittsburgh, Pennsylvania: Aluminum Company of America, 1948.

GOULD, MARY EARLE. *Antique Tin and Tole Ware.* Rutland, Vermont: Charles E. Tuttle Company, 1958.

————. *The Early American House.* Rutland, Vermont: Charles E. Tuttle Company, 1965.

————. *Early American Wooden Ware.* Rutland, Vermont: Charles E. Tuttle Company, 1962.

GRAHAM, ALBERTA POWELL. *Washington: The Story of Our Capital.* New York: Thomas Nelson & Sons, 1953.

HANKENSON, DICK. *Trivets*. Maple Plain, Minnesota: Dick Hankenson, 1963.

Home-Making and House-Keeping. New York: Butterick Publishing Company, 1889.

HOPKINS, ALBERT A. *Scientific American Handy Book of Facts and Formulae*. New York: Munn and Company, Inc., 1921.

Illustrated World Encyclopedia. New York: Bobley Publishing Company, 1965.

The Improved Housewife. "By a married lady." Hartford, Connecticut: Richard H. Hobbs, 1843.

JEFFERY, C. W. *The Picture Gallery of Canadian History*. Toronto, Canada: Ryerson Press, 1942.

JENKINS, DOROTHY H. *A Fortune in the Junk Pile*. New York: Crown Publishers, 1963.

KAUFFMAN, HENRY J. *American Copper and Brass*. Camden, New Jersey: Thomas Nelson & Sons, 1968.

LANTZ, LOUISE K. *Price Guide to Old Kitchenware*. Hydes, Maryland: Louise K. Lantz, 1965.

LICHTEN, FRANCES. *Folk Art of Rural Pennsylvania*. New York: Charles Scribner's Sons, 1946.

McCLURE, ABBOT, and HAROLD D. EBERLEIN. *House Furnishing and Decorating*. New York: Robert M. McBride and Company, 1914.

MOORE, ALMA CHESTNUT. *How to Clean Everything*. New York: Simon & Schuster, 1952.

NUTTING, WALLACE. *Furniture Treasury*. New York: Macmillan Company, 1954.

SLOANE, ERIC. *ABC Book of Early Americana*. New York: Doubleday & Company, Inc., 1963.

SMITH, CARLOTTA NORTON. *The Homemaker: Her Science*. New York: P. F. Collier & Son, 1905.

SPRACKLING, HELEN. *Customs on the Table Top*. Sturbridge, Massachusetts: Old Sturbridge Village, 1958.

STEVANS, PROFESSOR C. M. *Standard Home and School Dictionary*. New York: Leslie-Judge Company, 1911.

THORNBURG, VIRGINIA B. *Thornburg's Price Pointers on Primitives*. Privately Printed, 1956.

TUNIS, EDWIN. *Colonial Craftsmen*. New York: World Publishing Company, 1965.

TYREE, MARION CABELL. *Housekeeping in Old Virginia*. Louisville, Kentucky: John P. Morton & Company, 1879.

The University Encyclopedia. New York: P. F. Collier & Son, 1902.

VANDERBILT, CORNELIUS, JR. *The Living Past of America*. New York: Crown Publishers, Inc., 1955.

WELLS, RICHARD A. *Manners, Culture and Dress of the Best American Society*. Springfield, Massachusetts: King, Richardson & Company, 1894.

The Wise Encyclopedia of Cookery. New York: Wm. H. Wise & Company, Inc., 1953.

WOLCOTT, DUNCAN B. "Fact Sheet on Old Pewter Ice Cream Mold Collection of Duncan B. Wolcott." Cuyahoga Falls, Ohio. Privately Printed, n.d.

The World in Your Garden. Washington, D.C.: National Geographic Society, 1957.

WRIGHT, RICHARDSON. *Inside the House of Good Taste.* New York: McBride, Nast & Company, 1915.

———. *The Story of Gardening.* New York: Dodd, Mead & Company, 1934.

OLD CATALOGS

Biddle Hardware Company. Philadelphia, Pennsylvania, 1910.

Bristol Ware. Sherwood Brothers Company, New Brighton, Pennsylvania, n.d.

Building with Assurance. Morgan Woodwork Organization, Oshkosh, Wisconsin, 1921.

Iron Clad Manufacturing Company. New York, 1890.

Sears, Roebuck & Company. Chicago, Illinois, 1905.

Syracuse Stoneware Company. Syracuse, New York, 1896.

United States Stamping Company. Portland, Connecticut, 1883.

The Van Heusen-Charles Company. Albany, New York, 1898.

Vermont Soapstone Company. Perkinsville, Vermont, n.d.

Walker, F. A., & Company. Boston, Massachusetts, 1886.

OLD MAGAZINES

American Cookery

American Magazine

Boston Directory

Century Magazine

Delineator

Good Housekeeping

Harper's

Harper's Bazaar

The Iron Age

The Ladies' Home Journal

The Ladies' World

McClure's

Munsey's Magazine

North American Review

People's Home Journal

Saturday Evening Post

Woman's Home Companion

CURRENT MAGAZINES

The Antiques Journal. Kewanee, Illinois.

Hobbies. Chicago, Illinois.

Spinning Wheel. Hanover, Pennsylvania.

Index

Numbers in italics refer to illustrations.